DOING A NEW THING?

Doing a New Thing?

Seven leaders reflect on the past,
present and future of the house
church movement

Brian Hewitt

Hodder & Stoughton
LONDON SYDNEY AUCKLAND

Dedicated to the memory of my parents Les
and Connie who taught me the value of a
selfless life.

British Library Cataloguing in Publication Data
A record for this book is available from the British Library

ISBN 0 340 63013 2

Typeset by Hewer Text Composition Services, Edinburgh.
Printed and bound in Great Britain by
Cox & Wyman Ltd, Reading, Berks.

Hodder and Stoughton Ltd
A Division of Hodder Headline PLC
338 Euston Road
London NW1 3BH

Contents

Introduction

The year is 1970. In the rural surroundings of an idyllic Devon village, Arthur Wallis is a man with a restless spirit.

A writer of international renown, he has been immersed from childhood in the stories of revival. Having returned from New Zealand, a country itself in the throes of a move of the Holy Spirit, Arthur now finds himself frustrated by the mediocrity and formality of much of the British church scene. From his many years of Bible study, he knows how different the New Testament church was, in terms of its power and its effectiveness, from its present-day counterpart.

Yet for Arthur Wallis, his is not merely a sentimental longing for the good old days. More and more he has become gripped by the conviction that the final days in world history would be climaxed by a series of shattering events in which the church would once again be thrust onto the centre stage. Such cosmic upheaval, he has concluded, would in turn usher in the return of Christ. He simply has to tell a few friends about it.

The resultant series of meetings at Arthur's home was to become pivotal in the development of what has become known by a variety of names, including the house-church movement, reflecting the origins of some though not all of the fellowships, the Restoration movement, and latterly the 'new' churches.

But that was not all. In America, an unconnected discipleship movement, centred around a group of men in Fort Lauderdale, Florida, had embarked on a similar agenda, though with different methods and outcome. And in Britain, new churches, often called 'fellowships', had begun to spring up, founded by men who were largely oblivious to what was happening elsewhere. Whilst Arthur Wallis would become a father figure to the ever widening group, it seemed clear to many that a hand mightier than Arthur's was at the helm.

Diverse in background, unequivocally charismatic, yet able to reach the middle classes in a way that the Pentecostal churches had failed to do, the leaders of the new churches all shared the same goal: the rebuilding, or 'restoring' of the present-day church to its New Testament splendour. And they shared the same conviction: that God was actively at work in the last days, to bring this rebuilding to pass. Those Christians who had come to believe that a period of lukewarmness and backsliding in the church would be a sign of the nearness of Christ's return were wrong – the era of the apostle, not the day of apostasy, was at hand.

Twenty-five years later, as the second generation of the new churches beckons at the door, it is perhaps time to evaluate both the history and the legacy of what has arguably been the most important development in British Christianity for a generation, and to hear from those who have been to the fore during that time.

Writing this book has been a labour of love. It also reflects something of my own spiritual journey during the last fifteen years, a journey which has been shared by many Christians in Britain.

After years of virtual standing still, the church has pulled up the tent pegs and begun to march. We may not yet have reached a land flowing with milk and honey, but we are certainly no longer camped in the desert.

The book is written then both for those within the new churches, for whom the personalities and events may be familiar, and for those like myself, who while not members of new churches have nevertheless been challenged – sometimes painfully – by new-church theology and practice. In addition, it is offered to the wider body of Christ in the hope that its readers will sense the same inspiration of the Holy Spirit as I have experienced in preparing the manuscript.

I first met Gerald Coates, Roger Forster, Terry Virgo, Peter Fenwick and Arthur Wallis during an eventful period as editor of *Redemption* magazine. The inclusion of interviews with several house-church leaders was not universally appreciated. My interview with Gerald, which forms the skeleton of a chapter in this book, threatened to drown us both in hot water! At a time of deep suspicion and defensiveness, the input of Arthur and Terry was only slightly better received. Five years later, the house-church theology concerning the church, the importance of apostles and prophets, and even the second coming of Christ, has become standard teaching in large swathes of the Pentecostal and charismatic movements – at least unofficially. The bricks have been turned into bouquets. Such is the nature of prophetic journalism!

Through their songs and seminars, the new churches have shaped many fellowships around the country, who have looked for suitable bottles in which to safeguard the new wine of the Spirit. Yet as the candid comments of seven of its leading men show, the movement has had to endure pain, turmoil and schism in the process. The brothers, with whose co-operation this book was written, are no cosy cartel. Having begun to build close relationships with each other in the 1970s, they found themselves largely at odds in the 1980s. The significant development of the 1990s is one of new relationships being fostered, but within a wider constituency of the body of Christ, and with the humility which the pain of previous failure often brings.

It is impossible not to detect recent changes of emphasis. Experience, wisdom and hindsight have combined to produce a pragmatism that is endearing to some (Gerald perhaps?), but unnerving to others (definitely Bryn!). Are the new churches becoming less radical? Are the other churches catching up? Or is God's agenda for the 1990s changing?

Only time will tell whether the 'new' churches will age with the passage of years. It's a concern that occupies the mind of men such as John Noble. New-church leaders are aware that church history is not in their favour. Today's radicals so easily become tomorrow's reactionaries.

But for now the familiar house-church agenda remains buoyant, if a little bruised. Readers will find it restated with passion and conviction. Like me, they will warm to the personalities behind the terminology. For those unfamiliar with the house-church scene, be sure to read Bryn Jones' explanation of the Kingdom of God, the rule of Christ on the earth through his church; it is this sense of mission and purpose that has given the movement its dynamic. And don't miss what Gerald Coates has to say on the law and grace argument that dominated and divided the brothers in the 1970s. Are Christians really to be trusted to live according to the leadings of the Holy Spirit rather than the scriptures? And be prepared to be shocked as Tony Morton and others make out the case for Christ not returning to the earth – or at least not yet. This emphasis on what must be done on the earth prior to the second coming is in many respects the starting point for anyone wishing to understand what the house-church movement is all about.

The proponents of Restorationism believe strongly that

God's plans will not be frustrated by an ineffective church. Rather he is busily putting the pieces together for those events of global proportions that will 'fill the earth with God's glory'. And despite many good reasons for turning his back on the church, God is actively at work raising up those ministries of apostles, prophets, pastors, teachers and evangelists that will restore the church to a condition in which it can be used as God's tool to usher in the Kingdom of his Son. Of that, the new churches and their leaders still have no doubt. Arthur would have been pleased.

Chapter 1

Bryn Jones: New-church visionary

In the packed auditorium, you can cut the atmosphere with a knife. There is a total hush among the several thousand people present. For most of them, this is the highlight of the week. The person they recognise as their leading apostle is sharing the vision for the next few years.

It's a typically stirring speech, and the crowd is loving it. Neither a temporary PA fault nor the frequent applause can disturb their concentration. Bryn Jones apologises for 'almost' getting excited as he relates the visions and dreams that have shaped his life, firstly as a teenager in his native South Wales, and later during a period of ministry in South America. And still the visions come. Is it the third or fourth? But who's counting? What the crowd doesn't know is that within thirty minutes, Bryn is going to share with them his present-day vision, which if fully implemented, will involve a financial commitment of four million pounds. In addition hundreds of families will be asked to consider uprooting their homes and lives in order to become part of the new fellowships that Bryn and his team want to plant.

It would be easy for the onlooker to be cynical. Is Bryn softening his audience up? Yet one thing is certain. Few men in Britain today have the charisma and ability to communicate vision and faith as Bryn does. Not for that reason alone, he occupies a unique position in the house-church scene in this country.

Born just a few months after the outbreak of war in 1940, Bryn spent a great deal of his childhood with his grandmother. Like the New Testament Timothy, he found himself coming under the godly influence of both his grandmother and mother. His grandmother's home had previously been used by the apostolic movement for cottage prayer meetings, and his great-uncle was an elder of that church. Though not born-again at the time, Bryn's mother was a God-fearing woman. Forty years later his memory of seeing her on her knees remains indelible.

'Like Cornelius, my mother was very God fearing. She attended a Baptist church in Aberdare. I can still see her praying morning and night by her bed. She seemed to be on her knees an awful long time. I used to think, "What on earth is she praying about for so long?" And I always thought that it was probably about me!'

New beginning

Bryn found the Lord in his early teens in the spiritual stirring that came to Wales following Billy Graham's visit to Haringay in the mid-1950s. A friend invited him to the local chapel, and on the way home challenged him to read Acts chapter 2. Bryn was actually more intent on listening to Elvis Presley at the juke box in the Italian cafe. But he went home, opened his mother's Bible and began to read what his friend had suggested.

'When I reached verse 21 – "whoever calls on the name of the Lord shall be saved" – I stopped. I knew that was what I needed. I didn't know how to pray, but I followed the scripture and called out aloud for God to save me. I dissolved in tears as God's presence filled the room. I knew that my prayer had been answered.

'The next day, I went over to the chapel and told the minister what had happened to me. From that point things moved very rapidly. The Christians in the valleys believed strongly that you had to believe in your heart and confess with your mouth. Consequently I was soon sharing my testimony in the open-air meeting.

'I was still only sixteen. In the prayer meeting, the nearest person to me in age was 45, but those godly men discipled me in the ways of God – they called it being "taken under wing".'

In 1957, Bryn was baptised in the Holy Spirit in the Aberaman Assembly of God under the ministry of William Hartley. At the time there was still a great deal of antipathy towards Pentecostals, and enormous prejudice against speaking in tongues. Nowadays you might be called a charismatic or a classic Pentecostal. In those days, if you spoke with tongues you were just of the devil! Within a month Bryn had been virtually excluded from the Baptist chapel for having become, among other things, a 'magician of Pharaoh'!

He began to fellowship at a small Pentecostal church in Pen y Waun. It was here he took his first steps in the things of the Spirit. He had already been schooled in such areas as prayer and godly living, but now Bryn was being exposed to the supernatural world of miracles and healings. And of prophecy that went right to the heart. There was a tremendous desire for revival in the valleys at that time. All-night prayer meetings were a feature of many churches, as a hunger for God gripped the believers: a neighbouring church had been having prayer meetings every night for almost a year. Bryn's own assembly met at least three nights a week to pray for revival. Eventually the pastor put a discipline on him in order to help his mother. He had to stay home one night a week!

While still in his late teens, Bryn began to feel a call to

preach, and a desire to go to Bible college. He enquired
of his pastor where he might enrol and was pointed
towards the Pentecostal college in London, though with
the rider, 'Don't go there unless you're sure that's where
God wants you.'

Inner voice

In fact it became fairly clear as time went on, that Bryn's
training for ministry lay in another direction. Having heard
about the faith ministry of Rees Howells, Bryn travelled
down to Swansea Bible College. As he walked in the
Italian gardens overlooking the sea, he felt God speaking
clearly into his heart: 'Ask of me and I will give you the
heathen for your inheritance, the uttermost parts of the
earth for your possession.'

Bryn had no money for the fees, but it was agreed that
he could enter the college on a 'faith basis', and learn how
to trust God to supply his needs.

'The three years I spent at Swansea were tremendous. To
be honest, I didn't receive a deep grounding in theology; it
wasn't that sort of college. And although it had a heart for
world missions, its strength wasn't missiology. What I did
learn however, was a deep devotion to God and the power
of corporate prayer. During my three years there, I cannot
recall a single day when we had less than three hours prayer
together. We were taught to pray through to the place
where you knew God had heard. When you knew he had
heard – whether it was for a tube of toothpaste, a pair of
shoes or even a car – then you were sure of the answer.'

Coming rain

One day, as the students met for devotions before lectures,

the Holy Spirit fell on those who had gathered. People were smitten across the room. Bryn opened his eyes and saw a vision of fine rain coming down the hills. As it continued on and on, he felt the Holy Spirit say, 'I will pour out my Spirit upon this land – and this time I'll never stop!' A year later, the same thing happened. The vision that Bryn saw and the events of that day still move him as he shares them: they have been an obvious source of motivation throughout his life and ministry.

Suddenly he saw a map of Great Britain. Small flames began to ignite in towns and cities around the country. Eventually they became so numerous that the whole map caught fire. What started in scattered places joined up until the whole nation was totally ablaze. Bryn started to speak and pray in tongues until the anointing subsided and the vision disappeared. He went for a walk in the same Italian gardens where God had spoken to him previously. As he meditated on this second vision an Ethiopian girl came running up, speaking in her own language. Naturally, Bryn didn't understand a single word.

'But you were speaking in my language earlier,' she insisted. 'You were talking about how God would cover the land with rain and that fires would burn in great revival throughout the nation.'

'Thank you Lord,' Bryn whispered, 'for all that you are going to do in our country.'

'I don't have to listen to sermons on revival to keep me believing it. I know that the biggest one ever is coming in our lifetime. I have never doubted it since.'

It was during his time at Swansea Bible College that Bryn met and shared a room with Reinhard Bonnke, who later founded Christ For All Nations (CFAN), and who now regularly preaches to tens of thousands of people in Africa. The two have kept in contact since.

First steps

Following a period of ministry in Cornwall, Bryn travelled
to France with Operation Mobilisation, before returning
to Britain with a romantic attachment to George Verwer's
secretary! Even in those early days, he was already beginning to think through his own ministry and calling. Three
things were already fairly clear in his mind: he had an
overwhelming compulsion to preach the gospel, a call to
the nations of the world, and a burden to plant churches.
Bryn has always seen himself as a pioneer, a role that
is generally attributed to him within the house-church
movement. Before that however, there would be many
learning experiences. The following anecdote was supplied
by *Restoration* editor, Roger Day. The speaker is Bryn
himself.

'I remember when I discovered in the Bible that the
gospel message includes divine healing. I was with two
other brothers on an evangelistic team in Norfolk. In my
enthusiasm I got a megaphone, stood in the town centre,
and started announcing divine healing meetings.

'"Bring the blind, halt, withered, and dead", I urged,
though I'm glad they didn't take me up on the latter! I
woke up the next morning covered in a red rash. My face
was bloated out and my eyes were half closed. We sent for
a nurse who said it must be some sort of allergy. I tried
everything to get rid of it, including looking at myself in
the mirror and rebuking what I could see, but to no avail.

'The next morning Derek, one of the other two brothers,
woke up to find his head was stuck in one position because
of a stiff neck. We again sent for the nurse, who said it
would take a few days to clear up.

'On the day of the meeting, Bob was the only one still fit.
He suggested that he should be the front man and the two
of us remain in our seats. We readily agreed. Fortunately

the meeting was scheduled for a Methodist church with a high pulpit. People would need a pair of binoculars to see what we looked like!

'That afternoon we went to the beach for one last publicity drive. Bob was telling people about the divine healing meeting that .evening when a wasp stung him. Within hours his arm had swollen up so much that he had to wear a sling. So the three of us went to the meeting that evening, me covered in a rash, Derek with his head stuck, and Bob in a sling. The first woman to arrive was in a wheelchair and used crutches to get to her seat. We decided to postpone the meeting.

'Within about three days, when our various ailments had disappeared, we were really ready. We decided to find the disabled woman and "give the devil a black eye" by raising her out of the wheelchair. We discovered that she lived in a house next to the church. When we arrived we stood around the woman, who had a little kitten on her lap, and began praying. I said, "I know what this is. It's a spirit of infirmity." So I said to the spirit, "In the name of Jesus Christ come out of her." With that the kitten did three leaps in the air – and dropped dead. I think I must be the only preacher who, on his first divine healing crusade, succeeded in killing the cat! I might add that the woman didn't seem to improve either.'

Fresh challenge

About this time Bryn met Guyanese-born Philip Mohabir, who was seeking to reach out to the new Black communities of London. In 1964 along with their wives they decided to set sail for Philip's home country to evangelise. It was only through a casual conversation with a British diplomat during the boat trip, that Bryn discovered that he was not heading for an idyllic Caribbean paradise.

'What have you done wrong?' asked the diplomat in an off-hand manner.

'I don't understand,' Bryn replied.

'Well I know what I did wrong, to be sent to the last outpost of the British empire,' came the reply. 'I was just wondering what you did wrong.'

Bryn and Edna Jones spent two-and-a-half years evangelising in Guyana. It was to be a time of deep reflection in Bryn's life concerning the nature of the church. A time also to reflect on the influences that had shaped his life until then. And a time to be challenged by a Muslim mufti.

'The Pentecostal men who I met in my early days, used to drum it into me that Pentecost was an experience, not a denomination. "We are a movement," they would say, "not a denomination." They were fiercely non-denominational.

'I was also influenced in my study of the church by certain books that I read, in particular a book by an Anglican missionary Rowland Allen, called *Missionary Methods – St Paul's or Ours?* In it he pointed out that in the early church, the apostles and prophets spearheaded an advancing people. He could find no reason why those ministries had disappeared from the church, and argued powerfully for the need to move away from bureaucracy and to rediscover the gifts and callings of the Holy Spirit.

'One of my teachers at Swansea, Ieuan Jones, had been strongly influenced by a similar teaching of Watchman Nee on the church, while a missionary in China.'

Almost from day one therefore, Bryn had been thinking through radical issues concerning the church of Jesus. As a result, he has not, since those early days, operated within a denominational structure. It seemed to him that while the church was made up of God's people, the denominations were made up by God's people, often as a result of personality differences. He had learned from the early conferences of Austin Sparks in London, that the true nature of the church is diametrically opposed to the church we see.

This was brought home to him by a Muslim mufti in Guyana. Surrounded by students of the Koran, he asked Bryn one day, 'How many gods have you Christians got?' 'Why, one of course,' came the swift reply. 'Not so,' he retorted. 'You have a Baptist god, a Salvation Army god, an Assembly of God deity etc.'

Bryn was stung and challenged by his mocking question. How could the church of Christ reach the ends of the earth with a gospel of 'one Lord, one faith, one baptism', which by the time it was packaged, had more varieties than Heinz soup?

When he returned to Britain from South America in 1967, Bryn knew that he needed to find the answers to these questions. The answers would shape the rest of his ministry.

Home group

In 1972, Arthur Wallis invited five brothers, including Bryn, to spend several days at his Devon home to pray and look at the subject of Bible prophecy. By this time Bryn, who had come to know Arthur through conferences, had moved to Bradford to lead a small independent fellowship. Bryn was the only one of the seven brothers featured in this book who was present at the first meeting, therefore his recollection of what took place is particularly significant. In addition to Arthur and Bryn, those present were Huw Thompson, Graham Perrins, Pete Lyne and Dave Mansell. As they sought to reach common ground in areas of theology, they experienced, according to Bryn, 'a visitation of God in prayer'.

*   *   *

'As we sought God together, it was as if we became immersed in a sense of oneness. Our differences of opinion seemed to melt away. All of a sudden we felt as one. We no longer had to strive in order to reach common ground. Rather we felt knit together with a common goal and destiny. Few if any of us understood the ramifications of what was happening to us. We just knew that we were experiencing a powerful manifestation of God's Spirit. Day after day there were strong prophetic utterances, and a deepening sense of excitement.

'During this time, the emphasis changed dramatically. We had gathered to discuss what the Bible had to say concerning the end times, particularly with regard to the nation of Israel. But suddenly we were being gripped by the Kingdom of God, not in respect of Israel – but the church! A vision of who the people of God really were dawned upon us in a fresh way.

'Up till that time, each of us had been working in an independent ministry. God showed us that in the body of Christ there was no place for independence. Relationship was firmly established on the agenda. We left Arthur's home changed men, humbled by what we had experienced, excited by what had been revealed to us, and knowing that we first had to work things through in our own relationships if we were to achieve a wider credibility.'

From the outset, it became fairly clear to Bryn and the other brothers, that the outworking over the next years of those momentous days in Devon was going to be difficult. The events that ultimately led to an acrimonious division between the group of leaders have been chronicled elsewhere, and will be touched upon at various points in this book. Suffice it to say here that one of the main areas of disagreement concerned the extent to which the teaching of Christian liberty should be taken. This produced attitudes and deep-seated positions which culminated in an inevitable separation. As rumours abounded, and were often sadly passed on by Christians without being substantiated, the name of Bryn Jones began to receive more than its share of flack. As the generally acknowledged leader of the emerging group, Bryn became a subject of controversy, with the name Bradford becoming a symbol of the new movement. It didn't help that at about that time, an off-beat religious leader in the USA had persuaded scores of his followers to commit suicide. His name? Jim Jones. And the place? Guyana! Would Bradford, some asked, become the next Jonestown?

Bryn is not exactly known for his timidity. What some see as strength, others would view as stubbornness. But as he reflects on those early days, it is clear that disappointment and frustration are etched in his memory.

Wrong step

'I felt at the time that it was a mistake to widen the group of brothers too soon. Some of the things we were seeing were so radical that we needed to proceed slowly. As strong men we had to learn how to submit to each other without compromising our convictions. We paid dearly for those mistakes, and for our theological immaturity. We were using terminology which we had not really thought through. We had a skeleton without flesh, and as a result many people assumed we were in error.

'Without doubt the greatest single hindrance was the church at large. Whenever God moves in a fresh way, it seems that those who are in the middle of it always get hit by everyone and everything outside of what is happening. It is as if Christians automatically want to kill dead any

new move of God, instead of saying, "Let's explore what
is happening together."

'An example of this is the whole issue of discipling,
which became such a source of controversy in the United
States. The brothers in Fort Lauderdale who were moving
along similar lines to ourselves developed a practice of one-
on-one shepherding in which everybody was responsible
to one other person. We never had that. Our discipleship
concepts were rooted much more in a system of elders who
were responsible for training and caring for the people
of God. This would often be in a small group or home
situation.

'Some people who moved in international circles and
were aware of the American model, equated it with
what we were doing. Consequently we found ourselves
under attack for something we weren't doing. Because
we believed and taught that Christians should be under
authority, we were labelled as the "pyramid" church. Our
critics pressed us to be definitive about this, whereas we
were just moving along step by step, trying to put the word
of God under our feet as we went along. Maybe that sounds
naive, but when you are in the throes of something new,
you can't always work out at the time the full implications
of what you are saying. Therefore it is not difficult for
onlookers to pick holes. But those who assumed and wrote
that we were teaching about apostolic authority simply
because we wanted to be evangelical popes, conveniently
neglected to highlight the safeguards of authority or the
positive aspects of apostolic ministry.'

Biblical basis

'I have been teaching for over twenty years the essential
areas of covenant, apostles and prophets, eldership within
the Christian community, and biblical discipleship. During

that time, no one has ever tried to present an opposing view from the scriptures. The kick-back has always been alleged excesses or hurts. No one has offered an alternative explanation of those scriptures which have all too often been ignored. Are we to be blamed for searching the scriptures?

'Several times I have written to Christians who have published articles on us, asking where they got their "facts" from. They never phoned, wrote, or contacted me prior to publication. Such practices are shameful among Christians. Indeed they smack of the very areas that we have sought to expose, that is a lack of love and relationship, criticism and back-biting.'

Bryn sought God early on as to whether he should defend himself. He felt the Lord say that his friends didn't need that – and that his enemies wouldn't believe it anyway. He has therefore constantly refused to defend himself against allegations and lies.

Perhaps Bryn's biggest disappointment however was the break-up of the group of men that came to be known as the 'fabulous fourteen', and which had developed from the original 'magnificent' seven who had met at Arthur's house. It seems to hurt a little as he reluctantly admits that what led to the division was '75 per cent Satan's doing'. He is well aware of the weakness of a position that teaches the importance of Jesus' prayer for unity in John 17, challenges Christians to confront each other in their relationships, and yet seems to have fallen at virtually the first hurdle.

Advantage Satan

'I believe passionately that Jesus' prayer for the unity of the church will be fulfilled before his return. We did try for a long time to resolve our differences, but Satan found a ready ally in our immaturity, and particularly in our inability to handle setbacks. I don't think, however, that we can blame the devil for what happened among us: he merely exploited our weakness area. He took advantage of the landing strip of our immaturity, hastiness and belligerence.

'Having said that, two other things need to be taken into account. Firstly God has still worked to bring about an advance in his Kingdom despite the problems that hit us. Perhaps some men are now making greater headway for God than they would have if we had stayed together. That doesn't make division right; it simply makes God greater than our divisions.

'I remain convinced that the oneness for which Jesus prayed will become a reality. When that happens, we are going to see an unparalleled outpouring of God's Spirit in such a miraculous way that will devastate the kingdom of darkness. The two are linked inextricably. That's why I am passionately concerned for the restoration of the church. I want to see the devil and all his demons put to flight. Satan knows what is at stake and I believe that he pulled out all the stops in order to destroy the testimony we were seeking to bring.

'Do I throw in the towel, and ask for a juniper tree like Elijah because I lost the first round? No – this is round two. Satan will be the loser next time!'

During recent years, Bryn has devoted himself to serving the sixty or so churches in Britain that look to him for apostolic input. New developments have created changes. A new location near Coventry serves as the focal point and administrative centre for the group, now renamed Covenant Ministries. There is no doubt that the move to the Midlands is itself a statement of the vision and goals that Bryn and his team have in their sights for

Britain. But at a time when some of the other men are rebuilding links and relationships, Bryn appears to be ploughing his own furrow. How does he react to the suggestion that at a time of coming together through such activities as Spring Harvest and March for Jesus, he is in danger of being marginalised and isolated from the wider body of Christ? He won't like me saying it, but the question seems to slightly agitate him. Strong men are perhaps not always the most patient when it comes to criticism!

'We came together originally with a specific agenda. I'm not aware that there are any groups coming back together on the basis of those issues. If there were, then I would want to be included. But I'm not interested in mere interdenominational get-togethers. And I can't go along with the idea of getting together in order to show that we are unified. That kind of unity is bogus. I don't feel that I'm being marginalised. I feel it's God's agenda that is being marginalised.

'I used to belong to an evangelical fraternal in Bradford. One day I heard on Radio Leeds that we had been expelled from the fraternal for being a sect akin to the Jehovah's Witnesses. Today we have the largest congregation in the city, yet are expelled from the fraternal. The truth is that we have all too often been excluded – not exclusive!

'A well-known speaker called in to see me some time ago and asked why I had never spoken at a certain Christian holiday event which takes place each year. My answer was simple, and to him surprising: I had never been asked! People sometimes make assumptions that are wide of the mark. I am simply seeking to carry on with the agenda that we started in the 1970s. I believe that we can neither ignore that agenda, nor substitute our own. After all, the agenda is God's.'

Still on course

'I'm trying to stay on the track. If that sounds exclusive, it is not what I intend. No doubt others are trying to do the same. I'm sometimes asked, "Has the Restoration movement peaked? Has it lost its way?" My answer is that Restoration is about what God is doing. He knows what he has planned and he will bring it to pass. Sadly we have failed abysmally as a people of God. By and large, the church is not on God's track. It has rejected what we stood for in the 1970s. But I am convinced that it will have to come back. The church is still avoiding the issue of God's government and rule. However we will have to face up to it once again, because it's true.

'When we called for a restoration of divine order in the church, we were in fact calling for a return to the word of God. In recent years, many have rejoiced in the experience of the Spirit, but have made no effort to measure their activities and practices by the scriptures. Experience rules – but that is not OK.

'People have taken on board those things which can bring a measure of blessing, such as praise and worship and house groups. We have never had house groups as most people understand them. We saw them as a church in the home, something to advance the rule of God in the community. A house group on the other hand is a maintenance tool to look after the people who are already with you. But people don't stop to get hold of the theological definitions, they pick and choose what they find acceptable. By and large, anything that threatens the existing power structure of a church is resisted. I have had ministers come to me and say candidly that they do not believe certain teachings espoused by their denomination, yet they have refused to stand up and be counted. I'm afraid that at times, the pension and the manse take precedence over principle.'

Present plans

Covenant Ministries essentially consists of a core group of six or seven men with the back-up of other men and ministries. The group's name underlines the sense of agreement and mutual commitment that is still such a hallmark of Restorationism. According to Bryn, the men have covenanted together in order to achieve certain goals. At present these goals are primarily twofold. As you would expect, they are global rather than local.

In Britain their priority and task is to take the gospel to the 92 per cent of people who are unchurched. In particular the team has highlighted some of the under-evangelised cities, and rural areas in Western Scotland and North Wales. One of the adjustments they have made over the years is that they now go into a town with a view to taking the gospel, rather than to planting a church. If the gospel is received, the believers are gathered together in a home, with perhaps more people from elsewhere. That then becomes a church.

'In terms of the towns and cities of Britain, we have set ourselves a huge task: to ensure that by the year 2000, every major town has a strong Christian testimony. We would be foolish to believe that we can achieve this by ourselves. There are others who may not agree with all our theology or methods, but whose gospel is essentially the same as ours, and who have similar goals. We respect that and have no wish to compete. But my attitude can be summed up this way: I believe that the task will be accomplished by us all, but I have to work as if we are the only ones left.

'Our second task is to raise up prophetic testimonies in the community which by the quality of their life, challenge the non-prophetic institutionalised Christian church in this country. I don't mean a politically competitive challenge

but rather in a way that will force the church in Britain
to face up to and confront the issues which we believe are
high on God's agenda.

'Our first priority therefore is the battle against the
powers of darkness that keep people blind to the truth
of the gospel. The second is to engage those same spiritual
powers which are entrenched in so many of the Christian
institutions in our land.'

There are about sixty churches around the country linked
to Covenant Ministries, all of which are 'home grown'.
In addition, another four fellowships which were already
house groups, have established ties with Bryn and his
team. Significantly, Bryn turns down invitations from up to
fifteen groups each year who, in Restoration terminology,
want to relate to him. The reason, according to Bryn, is
simple: there are too many difficulties that occur when
working with existing churches. Such a policy marks Bryn
out from most other house-church leaders, and may be
yet another reason why the 'exclusive' label refuses to go
away from Covenant Ministries. To be fair, it also destroys
the myth – at least for the present – that house churches
do most of their evangelism within other churches. So
how does the 'relationship' between Bryn, his team and
the sixty or so churches operate, particularly when one
remembers that house churches have experienced as many
difficulties in the area of relationships as the rest of the
church?

'The churches linked to us are established under their own
eldership and operate locally as they feel best. We are
often accused of being a denomination, but with no central
headquarters, no tenets of faith, no property control etc.
I don't feel that accusation can be substantiated. Their
links to us are solely relational: it is an organic, spiritual
thing. I don't know of any denomination where that is the

case. Usually the links are with the movement itself, not the men of gift within it – that is the difference as far as we are concerned. Some years ago, God spoke to us that we were not to build on another man's foundation. Ever since, we have sought to be obedient to God in this area.'

Supporting role

'The churches who are committed to us, would see myself and my brother Keri as being apostles to them, and men like Alan Scotland and Dave Mansell as prophets. As such they welcome our input and ministry as spiritual fathers among them. Of course, it's the question of authority that interests people who are not part of us. We do exercise a degree of authority: for example, 90 per cent of the elders have been set into office by us. That doesn't mean that we appoint 'our' men. Rather we seek to recognise God's men within the group. We are a constant source of counsel and support to them.

'If you take no account of the relationship of love and trust that exists between us, you might suppose that our structure is highly authoritative and stifling. All I can say is that the people in our churches are the most liberated, "bound up" people I've ever seen! The truth is, and it is a vital point that is at the heart of our teaching on authority and submission, that it is those who are not under authority that are often bound up.

'Not everyone can cope with the issue of authority. After all, it is demanding and runs counter to the spirit of the age. Consequently people do sometimes leave us when it comes to facing the real issues of Christian discipleship. But people left Jesus in droves at certain points in his ministry. People who have left us, and have subsequently criticised us, have invariably had a problem with authority. The churches who are part of us don't see it as authority, but as a relationship between fathers and children. Until you explain it as authority, they see it just as relationship.'

Few house-church leaders have attracted the level of controversy that has gathered around Bryn Jones. Not surprising perhaps, since he has been the most prominent figure in the movement during the last two decades. As mentioned earlier, his name has become a by-word for the new churches, a synonym even for Restorationism. One cannot help but feel that he has been targeted, often unfairly, by those looking to pin the blame and responsibility on someone for every excess and deviation of those who claim to be restored!

Or perhaps it's because of the strength of Bryn's personality. Depending on how you view him, he's either self-opinionated or prophetic! And while he doesn't set out to court controversy, one gets the feeling that he doesn't mind it in manageable quantities. Perhaps it has even been a source of motivation and strength in itself.

Money matters

But if the question of authority and submission to leaders has been the biggest source of contention, particularly with regard to Bryn's group of churches, the subject of money comes a close second. The stories about money and the house churches are legion and usually they centre on whether members give freely or under compulsion. Bryn has long since got used to wild accusations about his own standard of living and of pressurising others to give large amounts of money to his organisation.

But with Bryn, other rumours have surfaced recently, linking him with American-style prosperity preaching. At

its worst, the teaching panders to the greed and material-
ism of Western Christians by encouraging them to expect
or 'claim' money and luxury items from God as a sign of
his love and favour. The invitation to give generously to
the teacher as a way of triggering God's own generosity is
never far away! Does Bryn really believe that God wants
all Christians to be rich in this way? There's a glint in his
eye as he begins his answer.

'Of course I believe in prosperity – but only as it is defined
in the Bible. What I don't believe in is poverty. I'm amazed
how many Christians have been taught to believe that
poverty is a blessing, and that wealth or physical blessings
are something to be embarrassed about.

'I've never yet met one poor person who said, "I'm so
blessed to be poor!" But I've met thousands who pray that
they might escape their poverty. And I can't find a single
scripture that tells me that poverty is a blessing to the poor.
I do read however that "poverty is the ruin of the poor"
(Proverbs 10:15).

'God has covenanted – or promised – prosperity to his
people. It's a matter of his honour. But that doesn't mean
that every Christian will have a Rolls Royce and a yacht.
Moffatt's translation of 2 Corinthians 9:8 is one that I find
helpful: "God is able to bless you with ample means, so that
you may always have quite enough for any emergency of
your own and ample besides for any kind act to others."

'Prosperity isn't what you have – it's what you have
access to. Jesus had nothing in his pocket, but he had
access to all that he would ever need and more to bless
others with. I can be prosperous, emotionally, physically,
and mentally even if I have no money. Money is not the
key to prosperity. There are many who have large amounts
of money, but who live in poverty.

'Most Christians will say that they agree with this kind
of prosperity, but in practice they are more comfortable

with the notion of poverty. Paul said that he knew how to be abased and how to abound, but many of God's people have only learned how to handle the former. That's why we need to emphasise and teach prosperity. The first step to prosperity is to believe that it is God's will for you.'

Bryn pauses for a while. His reasoned argument on this subject, as on others, is difficult to refute. He has the pained expression of someone who really can't understand what all the fuss is about. I'm beginning to wonder the same. Is Bryn merely the object of the kind of misinformed – or even mischievous – rumours that tend to surround those who pioneer new paths and methods? Is he perhaps a victim of the British pastime of denigrating its heroes? Perhaps the tendency of prophets to attract persecution is also true of apostles! Bryn is quickly on the offensive at the suggestion that his organisation, and especially its leaders, creams off money that ought to be used in local churches.

Open door

'I sometimes hear the accusation that we are secretive about finance. In fact, during each of the last twenty years or more, we have lodged an audited statement of our accounts with the charity commission. All of our accounts are handled by qualified accountants and are vetted by an outside firm. Anyone who wants to see our financial statements can obtain a copy from Companies House!

'It's also wrong to say that we receive tithes from the people. Rather, we are constantly asked by elders from the churches how they can get behind our apostolic efforts to advance God's Kingdom. Our answer has usually been to suggest that churches send a tithe of their own tithes, i.e. ten per cent of their income to Covenant Ministries.

'About 90 per cent of our churches now do that, though

at least a third of those are financially involved with our ministry well beyond that level of giving.

'We encourage pastors and leaders to tithe outside of their local church – but not to us! This money has become a fund that is available for use in needy situations. We will make recommendations, but do not control the funds. For example, we asked the elders to consider sending funds to support African pastors and as a result, £18,000 was sent out of the tithing account.

'My own salary is made up largely from the support of four churches, in addition to ministry gifts which I receive. Most of the brothers who do not pastor churches operate in a similar way. However, we do have an understanding, that if someone's total income does not reach £15,500, it is made up from a central fund. But most of us are prospering well beyond that.'

There's no denying that house churches produce committed people. And that those committed people are good givers. Covenant Ministries has a world missions budget of over half a million pounds a year. Part of this is devoted to a humanitarian programme called Help International. Projects which have been undertaken include a literacy programme in Zaire, a fully equipped maternity hospital in Zambia, and an aid distribution centre in Mozambique supplied by twenty-ton containers every six weeks. Nearer to home, a building has been purchased in Romania for use as a hospice for AIDS sufferers.

Hidden meaning

Alongside this is an evangelistic programme which operates in all of these countries. Eight men are currently supported in this ministry. It's all part of what Restorationists call 'bringing in the Kingdom'. That's a theme which runs both through their teaching and their songs. Church members are encouraged to enjoy 'Kingdom life', possess a 'Kingdom mentality', and in general to be 'Kingdom people'. But what do Bryn and the other Restorationists mean by that, and why is it so important in their thinking?

'The "Kingdom of God" refers first and foremost to God's rule over people. Whenever someone submits their life to God, they become a part of God's Kingdom. In that way his Kingdom is extended. Jesus left us in no doubt that his Father's Kingdom was not territorial like an earthly one; neither is it merely futuristic. Rather it is a present reality in the hearts of his people. We believe implicitly that the rule and influence of God over the peoples of the world is going to be vastly extended as we near the time of Christ's return. This will necessitate the pulling down by supernatural means of the kingdom of Satan which now rules over the hearts of people. And how is this to take place? Through the church of Jesus!

'This sense of the church's destiny has been a crucial hallmark of our message. We do not believe that Christ will return for a feeble, cowering people. We reject such a possibility unequivocally. Rather we believe that God is actively restoring his church in order to use it as a tool to extend his rule across the nations.

'In spite of the fall of mankind, God's commission to Adam remains: "be fruitful . . . fill the earth and subdue it. Rule" (Gen. 1:28). This process was begun in Christ, and is to be completed by the church, his body on earth. Unfortunately, Christians have consigned scriptures such as Philippians 2:10–11 – that every knee shall bow and every tongue confess Jesus as Lord – to a future age. As a result they shrug their shoulders in helplessness, and wait to be rescued from this present world.

'But God is concerned now about injustice and famine, about political decision-making and cardboard cities,

AIDS and drug abuse. In all the enormous upheaval that is taking place in the world today, and especially in Europe, we are seeing the strongholds of Satan being thrown down. At such a time we must not stand idly by; rather we must use the authority of Christ's name to do good works, cast out demons, heal the sick and destroy the works of Satan in our world.

'"If I drive out demons by the finger of God", said Jesus, "then the Kingdom of God has come to you" (Luke 11:20). In the same way, we are to be a prophetic people, bringing the present world order into submission to God's order and rule. That is our task prior to the return of Jesus.'

Waiting game

Here lies one of the distinctive areas of house-church theology. While most Christians have been taught to expect the return of Jesus at any time, most of the house-church leaders do not. Or at least, not yet. Not that the end times are unimportant to the house churches. Indeed it can be argued that the 'last things' are higher on the agenda of house churches than of many other Christian groups. The return of Christ and the closing of human history is not seen as an arbitrary decision to be taken by God, but as the final chapter of a plan conceived by him, revealed through Christ, and implemented by Jesus through the church.

Bryn himself believes that God's rule will ultimately extend over the earth in such a way that every institution of society will feel the impact. It ought to be said, however, that he backs away from the teaching of 'reconstructionism', which expects the Kingdom and indeed Kingdom people to take over those institutions. Whatever the rights or wrongs of the theology – and it is not short of critics – such a teaching has given the house churches that sense of vision and dynamic purpose that is unmistakable.

It has also brought the house churches into conflict with other Pentecostal groups, for whom the concept of a literal one thousand-year reign of Christ on earth has been sacrosanct. Not surprisingly, since Bryn and others do not believe in a millennium of peace on earth during which there will be a spiritual awakening among the nation of Israel, there has been a strong reaction both from Jews themselves and from what Bryn less than tactfully describes as a 'body of deceived evangelicals'.

'I don't think that I believe in a literal one thousand-year reign of Christ on the earth. I'm sorry if that's a wobbly answer, but I adopt the same attitude towards this as the "once saved, always saved" question. I believe implicitly that having been born again, nothing I will ever do will "unborn" me. The worst backslider is still a son of God as far as I understand, no matter how far adrift he may be. But on the other hand, I'm not infallible. So in case I'm proved wrong, I'm going to carry on walking righteously!

'Similarly I don't see the end times in terms of a literal millennium, followed by an outpouring of demonic activity which is then put down by the Son of God. Rather I see the second coming of Jesus as bringing in the final end to God's offer of redemption. It will be a time of conclusions and judgement. The saints will be raised and will share in this judgement.

'What the teaching of dispensations did, was to create another opportunity for the Jews to be saved during the millennium. If you were to take out the one reference to the millennium in the book of Revelation, it is not even inferred in the rest of the New Testament. So I would say that I'm absolutely certain there won't be a millennium until I read Revelation chapter 20!'

Stormy weather

In May 1991, *Restoration* magazine's editor Roger Day
published an edition entitled 'The Truth about Israel'.
Coming at the height of unrest in the Middle East and
in Israel particularly, it was bound to be provocative.
Correction, it was *meant* to be provocative! But then, no
one has ever accused Bryn and his team of expediency. The
basic premise of the edition was to re-examine the biblical
teaching concerning the Jews, and to challenge traditional
views concerning Israel. True to form, the notion of the
Jews and the nation of Israel as God's chosen people was
given short shrift. It has long been a plank of Restoration
teaching to interpret most Old Testament prophecies and
promises regarding Israel as being now applied to the
church. Indeed that had been the basis for those first
meetings of leaders in Arthur Wallis' home.

But the greatest provocation was to compare in tabular
form the apartheid policies of South Africa with those of
Israel towards its Palestinian neighbours, and to criticise
those Christians who seemed to close their eyes to the
injustices of the Israeli nation on account of its special
historic relationship with God.

The storm of protest, especially from the powerful
Jewish lobby and press, surprised even Bryn. But he
remains unrepentant – and one suspects somewhat enjoying the skirmish.

'We simply took the line that Jesus and Paul took, that
you must interpret the Old Testament with the keys of
the New. And we felt it was right for Christians to
know that at a time when South Africa was abandoning
its laws on apartheid, Israel was reinforcing them against
the Palestinians. When you only talk about Israel theologically, you have no problem. But when you apply
it on the ground, you become prophetic. And yes, the

prophetic always stirs things up because it gets to the root of things.'

Certainly Bryn, now in his mid-50s, has been getting to the root of things for the last twenty years. Along with Arthur Wallis, he has probably been the single most influential architect of Restorationism in Britain. Although not everyone has been able to work with him, he inspires deep affection and confidence among those around him. If, as some feel, he is being sidelined at a time when other groups are coming more into mainstream evangelicalism, he is unlikely to be moved. Bryn follows the cloud, not the crowd! He seems to work best with his back to the wall. After twenty years he's used to it. And the vision still burns brightly.

'I don't believe that in time we will inevitably become institutionalised just like any other denomination. I know that all the lessons of history point to that. But that is to make history more powerful than God.

'John 17 indicates that a generation will arise that will fulfil the prayer of Jesus. If we are not to be that generation, I believe we will leave things in a way that will see its fulfilment in the next. That it will come, there is no doubt.'

Chapter 2

Tony Morton: Thinker and theologian

The year is 1968. A young student home from college wanders into Liverpool's Protestant cathedral. But his mind is on the immediate, not on the eternal. Depressed and utterly unable to cope with life, he has already contemplated suicide. Heavily into existentialism, he had come to the conclusion that life wasn't worth living.

As he entered the Chapel of the Holy Spirit, the sun shone, highlighting the window of Christ praying in the garden of Gethsemane. Suddenly, Tony Morton was conscious of an inner voice speaking to him: 'He died for you – just live for him.'

A warm sense of God's peace filled his heart, and in his own words, Tony walked out of the cathedral a new man. He didn't know any Christians; but he knew God, and his life was immediately transformed.

He went out with his mates that evening, and calmly said to them, 'I won't be drinking with you tonight, I've become a Christian.' They thought it was the funniest thing they had heard all week! But Tony knew it was real.

What Tony did not know, however, was that over twenty years later, he would become the leader of an apostolic team in Southampton, which has had a major impact in that area for God. In addition to a city church that comprises 550 adults, the Cornerstone team has planted another thirty churches, and has invested greatly in both ministry and finance into many nations of the earth.

One of the first decisions Tony made following his conversion was to leave his business college training in London. For a number of months he looked after maladjusted epileptic children, before resuming his studies at Southampton University. On only his second day, Tony finally met up with an evangelical Christian. He pushed a tract into his hand, and told him in no uncertain terms that he needed to be born again! Tony knew none of the Christian jargon, but as the stranger explained to him what he meant, he was articulating what Tony had already felt.

Out and about

Tony joined the hottest group of believers on campus, and from that day on, began to involve himself heavily in evangelism both on the campus and throughout South Hampshire. For the following twenty years, his life has simply been a progression and extension of that. He is still heavily into evangelism, with a passion to bring to Christ people who need him as much as Tony did, and to see new communities of Christians raised up throughout the area.

Like so many other evangelical students in the city, Tony initially linked himself to the well-known Above Bar church, and its respected minister Leith Samuel. There he was exposed to the great teachings of the Reformed tradition – and to the debate between those who wanted to emphasise God's sovereignty, and those who were equally passionate about human free-will.

As a fairly new Christian who loved the Lord and just wanted to evangelise the lost, Tony struggled to come to terms with such issues, held as they were by men of deep conviction on both sides. But the age-old arguments between Calvinists and Arminians were about to be dwarfed by a crisis that would thrust him onto the centre stage of leadership in the city.

Missing link

'Although I was very active in evangelism, few people were getting saved. So I began to cry out to God for a real fruitfulness in my witness. I felt that I needed an extra dimension of power in my life that would both lead people to Jesus, and give me victory in my own life over sin. I had immersed myself in the Bible, but it was clear to me that my lifestyle did not express the freedom from sin, or the joy in the Lord, that I had read about in the New Testament.

'Then I met a few Pentecostals, who told me that I needed to be filled with the Spirit. At first I rejected this strongly as being unbiblical. But eventually I realised honestly before God that I was unfulfilled, unhappy and unsuccessful. I cried out in desperation: "Lord I don't know what the terms are – and I don't actually want to be filled with the Spirit – but come and do whatever needs to be done to me, so that I can really live this life for you."

'I was filled with the Spirit quite dramatically – but didn't speak with tongues owing to my fear of the demonic! It seems daft now, but at the time there weren't many role models around. After a few months, I realised that the Holy Spirit had not done me any harm, so I asked God to help me speak with tongues, which he did.

'My own experience of salvation and of being filled with the Spirit have made me wary of laying down rigid guidelines for everyone else. I would expect those who are filled with the Spirit to speak with tongues, but would not exert any pressure for it to happen immediately. Whether tongues are "initial" or "proceeding" evidence of the baptism, is not something I would live or die for.

'I would never say to anyone that it doesn't matter

whether a believer speaks with tongues. I believe that all Christians should be encouraged to drink of the Spirit and to manifest the gifts of the Spirit. If they do not, then in all honesty, they lead a deficient Christian life. I know this will offend some sincere, godly, believers, but that has been my experience.

'Similarly with evangelism. I will preach the gospel every day, but will rarely make appeals. From my own experience, I know that God can save people wherever they are, as long as they have the truth in them.'

Testing time

But for Tony personally, the baptism in the Holy Spirit was not only born out of a crisis; it led him into another. All of his friends – whether Arminian or Calvinist – disowned him for no other reason than his having experienced the Spirit's power. This sense of rejection left him devastated. It was surely in the purposes of God therefore, that shortly afterwards, Tony left England in order to spend a year of his language course in Spain. If he had any lingering doubts about the validity of his new experience in the Spirit, they were quickly expelled. Tony took a teaching job in order to pay his living expenses, but every spare moment was spent evangelising in Madrid. In the early 1970s, Spain was a very difficult place to evangelise. It was illegal at the time to preach in the open air. Students were rioting on the streets, in what was a distinctly dangerous environment. Despite the hardships, or perhaps because of them, he experienced an anointing of the Spirit beyond anything he had ever known in Britain. It also exposed him to the tremendous challenge of the nations and the sacrificial cost of missionary life. His year in Spain served to imprint on his life and ministry a burden for world missions which twenty years later remains as strong as ever.

On his return to Southampton, Tony soon discovered that the opposition in the Christian Union to 'neo-Pentecostals' showed no sign of weakening; but eventually, a few students in the Christian Union who were hungry for more of the Spirit began to draw together. An informal meeting on Saturday afternoons centred around worship, and what Tony recalls as 'the great theme of the 1970s across the face of the earth – the Lordship of Christ'.

They sang 'He is Lord', over and over again, until they were sure that he was! This only served to confirm to those who had stood against them, that they were unstable, heretical extroverts. The evangelicals in the city rejected them for being Pentecostal, and the Pentecostals rejected them for being intellectual! It was a bemusing time for Tony personally; all he wanted to be was a happy Christian in a local church, filled with the Spirit, and seeing God move in increasing power. Yet he now found himself in a corner.

In the beginning

It soon became clear that the only solution would be to establish a new fellowship in the city. So in March 1975, a group of about thirty 'fairly damaged people' started to meet in the only hall available, the Blind School. Tony smiles as he recalls the many jibes of those who were quick to see the irony of a people of vision meeting in a school for the blind!

'We didn't set out to be a threat, or to criticise anyone. We were just hungry for more of God than we had experienced in the churches around us. Ours was not a challenge to anyone; rather a reaction to the restraints that we had come across. Not surprisingly, all the waifs and strays came to us. An Anglican vicar friend of mine told me years later how amazed he was at the number of maladjusted people who came to our meetings, yet we had managed to win through to a sane and sound base. Looking back, it is a miracle. By his grace, God helped us to do something different.'

The group eventually settled on the title of Southampton Christian Fellowship, a name which later changed to The Community Church. During the first seven years of the fellowship, growth was of the order of 25–30 per cent per annum, remarkable by British church standards. In 1977, a small evangelical church which Tony and Arthur Wallis had helped into a greater understanding of the baptism of the Spirit, joined with SCF. By 1984, the total number of believers committed to the church had reached 900, of whom a quarter were children.

Ten years later, the overall numbers at SCC have somewhat declined. But if you're looking for evidence that the house church phenomenon in Britain has peaked, you won't find it here. Tony Morton may be recognised as an apostle in terms of ministry, but in terms of gift, he is first and foremost an evangelist. Apostles plant churches, while evangelists reach the lost. After almost two decades in the Southampton area, Tony retains a passion to do both. And to harness the gifts and talents of many of those who have joined themselves to the fellowship during that time.

Planting out

In 1977, Tony went full-time into ministry. Previously he had been an advertising account executive, but had given that up for the easier task of becoming a teacher! That had given him the school holidays to concentrate on building up the church and evangelising. However, having run a church of nearly 200 people, and held down a secular job, he found full-time ministry not challenging enough. The outcome was, that he began to plant new churches, first in Gosport and then in other towns on the Solent. From 1977 to 1981, he helped pioneer six new churches while leading SCC.

'In the mid-1980s our fellowship sent out groups of people to establish new works in several of the surrounding towns including Winchester, Eastleigh, Totton and Romsey. These were gifted people of quality, who were not always easily replaced. But we have always had a heart for evangelism and church planting. The burden that God gave me for the nations while I was in Spain as a young undergraduate, had to begin in Southampton. My burning ambition has never been to be the biggest church in Southampton, or to reach the magic 1,000 figure. Having said that, we have since bought a building in Southampton with 1,485 seats! We will be working hard in order to fill it, but not with the kind of blinkered determination that blinds us to God's wider plan for his church on earth.'

It was exactly this emphasis that brought Tony into contact with other house-church leaders in the mid-1970s. Feeling somewhat inexperienced and insecure, he drew alongside men like Bryn Jones and Dave Mansell and became deeply affected by the writings of Arthur Wallis. As it happened, the evangelical church which had joined up with Tony's group already had contacts with Arthur. Here was the father-figure par excellence that Tony had been searching for. His lifestyle spoke of integrity, and he possessed an equipping ability that could bring stability to the fellowship and to Tony and his wife. He asked Arthur, on a personal basis, to speak into his life and into the fellowship, and to challenge them with any inconsistencies he noticed.

'I needed someone more mature as a safety net, and as a

source of counsel. At that time, Bryn was developing his own ministry and was wanted as a speaker throughout the land, as someone who was fresh, anointed, and promising new things. But while there was an open door for Bryn among us, we saw him very rarely due to his popularity.'

Friend in need

Arthur however befriended the fellowship and its leader, bringing them the benefits of his Bible knowledge. Tony wanted him to move from his Devon home to Southampton, but at that time, *Restoration* magazine, of which SCF were co-owners, needed an editor; so Arthur moved to Bradford. Tony was deeply disappointed: he felt that he really needed Arthur, and that Bradford was already the focus of so much good ministry. So it goes without saying how delighted he was when Arthur came to Southampton some years later.

'I am deeply thankful to God that for the last seven years of his life, Arthur was a part of our local eldership and ministry team. Without doubt, Arthur Wallis has been the major formative influence on my life. Older and more mature than most of the other leaders, he had received an exposure to the revivals of the early twentieth century, both through his father and other contacts.

'Our vision does not centre on house churches. Rather it is focused on the supernatural power of God sweeping through ordinary people in salvation. We have a burden to see revival in our land. As we have fasted and prayed for revival over the last fifteen years, we have found ourselves becoming more burdened – firstly for the church, and then for the lost. However, this has simply been a stepping stone for what we really want, which is revival in the nation. What we are now in, is not what we are going for.'

Back to basics

When he established the fellowship in 1975, Tony purposely avoided the use of the word 'church'. He felt that he didn't know what a church really was, but he knew that he had to find out. He learned from Arthur that a revival has to be contained, otherwise it will leak away, and that a concern for the church, so important in the Restorationist agenda, must not become an end in itself. Rather it should be viewed as part of the preparation for revival, born out of the conviction that those who are converted to Christ at such times must be able to attach themselves to a church where they will grow spiritually. It is not enough for them to merely experience Christ and then be left, as it were, strewn across the country.

This concern for the church, and in particular, the emphasis on restoring the modern church to its original New Testament format, has been a major feature of the house-church movement. The argument is simple and irresistible: the church we read of in the Acts of the Apostles was a powerful, dynamic organism that 'turned the world upside down' (Acts 17:6). But its present-day descendant is on the whole neither powerful nor noticeable. The only remedy? Bring back the New Testament church, and New Testament results would surely follow.

From the early meetings of house-church leaders in the mid-1970s, the belief grew that not only did the church need restoring, but that God was actively at work to bring it to pass. In other words, restoring the church to its former splendour, was at the top of God's agenda for today. Through this 'bride without wrinkle', the rule or 'Kingdom' of God in the earth would be established. As in the days of the early church, the world would have to sit up and take notice.

Clear message

It is hardly surprising that Restoration teaching has been controversial and divisive. Its proponents are unequivocal and unbending. They know what they believe and they shudder at the idea of compromise. God is shaking and shaping his church as a prerequisite to revival. Christians need to submit themselves to 'present truth' and shake off their traditions and non-New Testament practices and attitudes. The church of God is moving on!

For Tony Morton, the goal of Restorationism has always been evangelism. He reacts swiftly to the suggestion that the house churches have been too introspective.

'We began by re-evaluating where we were, and by asking the question, "What is church life like in the New Testament?" It wasn't difficult to draw the conclusion that certain things were missing from our experience which had been present in the early church. We had been involved in certain religious proceedings which in themselves were emotionally pleasing. But the issue was, "How could we become more relevant to the non-religious people of the late twentieth century, without ourselves becoming irreverent?" The challenge was to find a way by which we could be easily approached by the world, but not consumed by it, or lose any Christian values.

'The major areas which we felt God redirect us were initially worship, fellowship and living in the grace of God, rather than the accepted norms that pass in most churches for spirituality or worldliness. We placed the emphasis back on what Christ had done for us, rather than on our own performance as Christians. Our desire was to establish the kind of reality and openness to each other, that seems to have been part and parcel of New Testament fellowship, but which has been sadly lacking in most modern church gatherings.

'We have sought to create a loving, honest-to-God environment, where people can face up to their weakness without feeling vulnerable. Our conviction from the beginning was that only after this time of preparation would the lost come into the church.'

True worshippers

'The same is true of worship. According to Acts 15:16, when the tabernacle of David is restored, "the rest of men shall seek the Lord". Worshipping God was seen in a new light; not just an enjoyable experience shared by God and his people, but rather a dynamic, powerful declaration of God's character and name which would break down the powers of darkness. When the church worships God in spirit and truth, people would surely flock in!

'With hindsight, it is now clear that while we touched something new in God, there was also a lot of naive idealism around. Our worship in the early days was hot – perhaps excessively so – but while we were growing, there was no queue of new people every Sunday afternoon asking, "What must I do to be saved?" There were however several people living nearby telling us to shut up so that they could get some sleep!

'One of the lessons the house churches have had to learn is that there is no easy formula to revival. Restoration is not a quick and painless route to blessing; anything that puts integrity and reality centre-stage is bound to provoke upheaval both in individuals and churches.'

One of the areas in which this upheaval was initially felt was that of submission and authority to leaders. Although house-church leaders tend to dismiss stories of 'heavy shepherding' as mythical, one should not ignore the havoc and pain that extreme discipleship teaching created in America, and to a lesser extent in Britain. Originally set out by Argentinian leader Juan Carlos Ortiz in his book *Disciple*, the practice of Christians being discipled by other Christians is not in itself unscriptural. But when pushed beyond biblical limits, the dangers are obvious.

Learn to obey

Tony and his fellowship never adopted Ortiz's model of Christians being overseen individually by an appointed shepherd. Indeed, most of the groups in Britain which did so, have long since disappeared into obscurity. But he did take on board the now classic house-church teaching, that you must be under authority in order to exercise authority. The underlying argument is persuasive: since God promises to give his Spirit 'to those who obey him', it follows that Christians will never be able to experience and express God's power in their life, until and unless they submit to that authority in every area of their life.

'Submitting ourselves to God's rule involves a willingness to obey those who exercise that rule in the church. Unless we are prepared to do that, it is pointless asking God to raise up apostles and prophets.

'The weakness of the personal shepherding model, is that it inevitably reproduces all the failings of the shepherd in the sheep. In Southampton, we see the whole church as a discipleship model through its lifestyle and commitments. That includes a leadership team that wields authority. We have had to walk a fine line on this, in order to guard against misusing authority. But don't forget that to under-use authority is as unscriptural as over-using it. On the whole, over a period of twenty years, I think that we have not made too many mistakes in this area. I can't recall anyone mowing my lawn at midnight in order to prove their submission to me as leader!

'That would be an abuse of authority. A leader is someone who lays down his life for Christ and the flock. It is a sacrificial ministry. We have never gone for an authority structure which elevates men to a position where they are either beyond question, or beyond access. On the contrary, we are just human beings who have been entrusted by God with certain gifts. But we are vulnerable, and need everyone's love and support to get to the end of the race.'

Different style

For several years, Tony and the Southampton fellowship were part of the Harvestime group of churches led by Bryn Jones from Bradford. In the terminology of Andrew Walker's book *Restoring the Kingdom*, this placed Tony at that time alongside Brighton's Terry Virgo in the 'R1' category of house churches. (The 'R2' group consisted mainly of churches linked to Gerald Coates, John Noble, and Peter Fenwick.) Indeed, the two south coast brothers were co-owners of *Restoration* magazine with Bryn Jones until withdrawing from that commitment and their close links to Harvestime in 1987. While the various brothers, Tony included, speak generously of each other, and clearly retain a genuine affection and respect for other leaders, it is not difficult to conclude that a difference of style was one of the major reasons for that decision.

'My involvement with Harvestime initially stemmed from my friendship with Arthur Wallis. Here were a group of prophetic, faithful men, who were doing their utmost to see Christ honoured in our land; there is no doubt about that. Bryn's approach was one of giving a strong lead.

Having a powerful prophetic gift, he was often the one who would hear from God. When he felt that he had heard from God, Bryn would go ahead.

'I have tremendous respect for Bryn. I know he takes a lot of flak – but he does not get it from me! Anyone who creates room, and does things, is bound to upset somebody.

'My style is different from that of Bryn however. My university training has meant that I'm more of a chairman who draws on the strengths of those around me. In saying this, I am not trying to compare favourably my style of leadership with that of Bryn or anyone else; rather to contrast differing ways in which men operate under God.

'Likening myself to a chairman within our leadership at Southampton does not mean that I simply follow the will of men. Rather I try to hear God through my peer level ministries, just as much as through the direct inspiration of the Holy Spirit to me personally. I am much more concerned about the team's final achievement than about who captained the team.

'Cornerstone Team originally consisted of Peter Light, David Damp, Arthur Wallis and myself. Now there is an inner group of men and women who would look to me for a word of wisdom, or authority in a crisis. But that has a very low visibility. We are friends who share a common burden to see the church scene changed and enriched in our land. By pooling our gifts and ministries, we hope to be able to make a contribution for the Lord as he leads us.'

In an attempt to emphasise this aspect of servanthood, the team took a conscious decision several years ago to change its name to Cornerstone Resources. What remains unchanged, however, is the commitment to plant new churches. A network of some thirty-five churches receives input from the team, most of which were planted directly by Cornerstone. Tony is at pains to point out that each of the churches is autonomous – that is, structured and led by local leaders – although the model is not one of independent churches, but of linked fellowships serving each other.

'Our aim is to produce strong churches. We believe humbly, that God has given gifts to the Cornerstone brothers that can be used to equip existing churches, as well as to establish new ones. There are certain key principles that undergird all we do.'

Serving first

'Firstly we believe that the apostolic team should serve the churches and not the other way round. When we plant churches, it is with the express aim of appointing local elders as soon as possible. We would cease to be involved in the oversight of that church at the earliest opportunity. Remember though, that our aim is to produce strong, mature churches. That can only become a reality through mature leaders. Once they are in place we would seek to help them to become sensitive to God for themselves. From then on we would rarely get involved unless requested to.

'I don't see the churches as being submitted to me personally. My flesh might well be interested in this kind of empire-building, but God wouldn't be. We believe in many elders or bishops over one church, not one bishop over many.

'Most of our churches started with just a handful of people. There are some that I don't serve at all now. They have grown up and no longer see the need. For a start I haven't got the time to relate closely to thirty-five churches. In practice, it is impossible to maintain a close relationship with more than about ten fellowships at any one time. And anyway, I want to get on and plant more churches. In order for that to happen, we must be able to entrust the work to local leaders who will shepherd the people of God. At that point I will become a source of counsel and back-up to them, if they want it.

'I don't want to contain churches within my particular group or brand name. They belong to God, not me. That's why we don't operate a system of strong authority. If an eldership wants to receive me as a gift to their church, then I will go and seek to be an equipper and a help to them. It's up to them to decide how and whether they implement that advice. I don't carry a big stick – neither do I think that they are necessarily in line for judgement if they decide not to put my advice into practice.'

Lower profile

'The change of name from Cornerstone Team to Cornerstone Resources was quite significant. Firstly because the team is no longer a fixed core of men; it has developed wider than that. And secondly, we have moved away from the concept of people being sent out with bishop authority. Rather we are equippers, a resource centre to the body of Christ. In a situation like that, the question of authority does not come high on the agenda.

'In the early years, we didn't visualise it becoming a loose kind of fellowship, but this has clearly been the direction in which the Lord has led us. This may mean Cornerstone having a lower profile, but we have to remember that our success is gauged not by how many churches depend on us, but how many grow to maturity in God through us. Like John the Baptist, we are quite prepared to decrease, if it leads to the increase of Christ in his body. Above all, I want to be an initiator, not an administrator or a mere sustainer.'

*   *   *

In a nation where Christian giving, at least financially, often ranges from the paltry to the mediocre, house churches have helped raise the issue of money to a higher place on the Christian agenda. Examples abound of huge offerings at special meetings, of expensive vehicles, property or jewellery being 'laid at the feet of the apostles'. Is all this part of the return to the New Testament church as some would say? Yet alongside such acts of benevolence, other stories persist claiming that money has been used to finance the lavish life-style of apostles and has been obtained under pressure from ordinary members.

Most of the accusations tend to centre on the practice of Christians tithing to other Christians rather than to their local church. Usually it is leaders who seem to be the main beneficiaries, often from other leaders who receive input and help in some way.

Certainly, in the early days of the house-church movement, there was an emphasis on leaders giving a tithe to other leaders, based on the Israelite practice of priests tithing to the High Priest. Since there were eleven tribes of Israel that tithed to the priests (the priestly tribe of Levi being excluded), there were consequently eleven tithes of a tithe that were reserved for the High Priest. In other words, he received 1.1 per cent of the gross national product as against the 9 per cent that the other priests were left to share out. If you wanted to be rich in Israel, then becoming the High Priest was as good a way as any!

Freedom in finance

Such teaching has obvious attractions for high priests. And distinct possibilities for apostles with big plans but small funds. It is perhaps a sign of a maturing movement that men like Tony Morton have abandoned the teaching in favour of a less legalistic, more relational approach to funding their ministries.

'We used to ask our churches to tithe into Cornerstone, but there were pitfalls. I found myself becoming the Chancellor of the Exchequer – balancing everyone's books, and rapidly becoming tied down with bureaucracy.

'Now we encourage people to tithe to their local church – not out of legalism, but out of a love for God, his servants, and a lost world. We simply ask those churches who relate closely to us, to receive our flow of information, and then to listen to God regarding any response. It's much better for them to pray and do what they feel God is saying to them, rather than contributing automatically to pooled funds.

'Local churches identify more easily when things are decentralised. There is more accountability when people know that it is the tithes of five postmen, two mechanics, three secretaries and a labourer that have sent their missionary to Africa.

'Of course it would be great if thirty-five churches each gave me £20,000 for missions each year; however, it would work against prayer and faith. As it is, we finance projects and send out ministries all over the world from Southampton. It's an immense commitment which on some days leaves us feeling slightly uncomfortable. But whereas a few years ago, perhaps a quarter of a million pounds was centralised each year, now it is hardly anything. But at least I've been able to vacate 11 Downing Street!'

Not that Tony can entirely extricate himself from such temporal matters. In a local church where last year's income was over £400,000, 25 per cent is given over to missions overseas, and projects in Great Britain.

It was in the mid-1980s that Tony, along with others,

felt that God was wanting to change the emphasis of the house churches. The prophetic thrust of the late 1970s had been well catalogued: apostles and prophets, praise and worship, submission and authority, fellowship etc. Those interested in such topics could easily obtain a back copy of *Restoration* magazine. Unless the house churches had something fresh to say, concluded Tony, they had better be quiet. Yet the change of prophetic emphasis was already happening. Before long it became clear that God was saying something about the church in the community. In a nation where abortion was endemic, and euthanasia on the horizon, a statement needed making. And Southampton was as good a place to start as anywhere.

Back to school

The first area that Tony and his team looked at was education. Having trained as a teacher himself, Tony was well aware of the issues involved in state education, as well as some of the pitfalls associated with operating overtly Christian schools. Finally however, the belief that Christians are themselves responsible for the education of their own children won the day.

So the church set about starting up a Christian school of its own. After several years in operation, and with numbers running up to 300 children, Tony looks back with satisfaction at what has been achieved in this area

'Academically, it is almost impossible to assess accurately. We don't have sufficient numbers for that. And it would be wrong to class us alongside public schools, or the independent sector in general. Initially, a school like ours attracts those who are not performing well at a state school. After all, why would parents withdraw their children if they were already performing well?

'For the first few years, this weighs against you. Some Christian parents are understandably cautious about making such vital decisions concerning their children's education. Others take the view that their children should be educated in a broader stream. So not all the children from our church attend our school.

'The school has certainly been valuable for those children who would not have attained good results in the state system. Those who would have performed well in state schools have done equally well with us. The benefit to them is that they have been able to study in a friendly, Christian ethos that doesn't work against the environment of the church and the home.

'We're not looking for the school to be an evangelical machine, where the children make a decision for Christ at seven, are taught to prophesy at eight, dance at nine, and are thoroughly bored by the time they are fifteen. Children from non-Christian homes do attend our school, and in that way it provides an easy door for evangelism. But the fundamentalist kind of institution which seeks to totally indoctrinate children frightens me. Our task is to present a biblical approach to issues like creation alongside the current view of evolution, and provide the children with the criteria by which they will have to make their choice.'

Hard option

The issue of choice is also at the centre of the other salt and light project that the community church has developed in Southampton. Last year 1,600 women were counselled at Firgrove Family Trust Centre, the first totally Christian-financed pregnancy programme in Britain. Led by a team of specialist counsellors made up mostly of doctors and women, Firgrove is a centre where those contemplating abortion are encouraged to choose the life option. Prior to setting up the project, a team of people was sent to various parts of the UK and to America to research it fully. A decision was also taken to locate the premises in a back street, so as to render it less visible – and therefore more approachable. As a result of counselling, a considerable number of abortions have been avoided. Equally important, Tony believes that the venture has an equipping role.

'We see Firgrove not merely as a role model of how Christians can be salt and light in the community, but also as a module that is available to the body of Christ in other areas. The project is not just about a bunch of enthusiastic do-gooders clumsily getting involved in a moral issue; it is a well-researched, highly professional presentation of the love of Christ to a hurting world. It is not enough for Christians to be protesting believers. Our clear and strong stand on moral issues must be linked to practical initiatives. That's why Firgrove has also run two homes for single mums.

'When we started Firgrove Family Trust, there were those who accused us of watering down our church planting vision in favour of social action. Even some whose voices I had learned to listen to felt that it was a wrong move. But we have to remember as leaders, that not everyone is gifted in church planting. Some church members have professional skills and expertise in a variety of areas. We cannot afford to waste this vast pool of talent that is available.

'From day one, we made a conscious decision to work with Christians from other local churches on this project. After all, Southampton Community Church does not have a monopoly on God's gifting. While we have taken a major lead, Firgrove is careful to present Christ, not a church. When people are won to Christ, they are introduced to whichever church suits them best.

'In the mid-1980s, I would not have envisaged a situation

where we would be working with other churches in this way. It's probably fair to say that house churches kept themselves apart – and were kept apart – from other churches. It's a sign of a new maturity on all sides that these barriers are now breaking down.'

Matter of choice

'House churches are not the answer for everyone. We ourselves are a group of middle class, fairly flamboyant people who have met the needs of a slice of the market. Others may prefer a type of Sunday morning meeting where expository preaching is central. Why should one be superior to the other?

'Hindsight is a terrific thing. When house churches started out in the mid-1970s, the attitude used to be, "God is restoring something new – everything else will be blown to pieces."

'With the gift of twenty years of observation, I don't now believe that is how God works. Rather, I believe that God blesses wherever there is obedience and faith. We are all working within blemished churches, which have both mature and immature Christians, with a variety of convictions on secondary issues. Despite all the discomfort that this brings, if we love God and believe him for things he has given us to do, we will achieve them. This is as true for someone in an Anglican, URC, Methodist or any other church.

'I'm not against denominations in themselves – though I'm not trying to create another one! But I believe that God will bless the denominations. It seems to come in cycles. Right now, I feel that the Anglicans will see once again a decade of great renewal.

'In the old days, house churches tended to rather sim- plistically interpret the "pure bride" as the new emerging churches. Everything else was categorised under various uncomplimentary names like "harlotry" or "Egypt". To be honest that was an arrogant attitude that still needs repenting of in certain areas. The truth is, that within many if not all denominations, there will be churches led by godly people who will implement godly standards within their traditional church structures. And they will form the "pure bride". On the other hand, there will be outwardly charismatic churches which will turn out to be nothing.'

One of the distinctive features of house-church theology has been its stance on the second coming of Christ. The emphasis has been on the church fulfilling the purposes of God on earth prior to Christ's return. Phrases such as 'Kingdom now', 'taking the land', and the application of many Old Testament promises concerning Israel in a way that sees their fulfilment in the church, have served to heighten the sense of destiny that house churches feel – and lessen the expectation of Christ's imminent return.

In the wings

For those Christians who have been taught to expect the Lord's sudden return at any moment, it can be somewhat disconcerting to be told that Christ's return is not now at hand. Is it not highly dangerous for Christians to lose sight of a belief that was certainly current in the early church? According to Tony, who admits to slightly hedging his bets on this issue, it is not so much a case of losing sight, but of regaining it. A church that is constantly looking upwards is a church that is failing to look outwards. The house churches, he argues, have rediscovered something of God's plan for the church, and of his heart for the nations.

*   *   *

'Jesus could of course return tomorrow. But it would seem more likely from the scriptures that he won't. Therefore we must do two things as Christians. Firstly we must shape ourselves to live the sort of faithful, enduring Christian life that believers have followed throughout the centuries.

'Secondly, we must plan a strategy for missions that will take the gospel to the ends of the earth. In this way, we can hasten the Lord's return.

'I feel so impoverished and broken when I travel to certain nations. I have been devastated for days when travelling in India. A place like New Delhi must be a major grief to God. After 200 years of missionary work there, life has little value. How are we to reach a mass of humanity that is so far removed from the realities of Christ and of the gospel?

'I'd love to go and plant fifty churches in India, but that would be a wrong strategy. Our task must be an equipping one. What the believers in Asia need from me are, for example, ten seminars on the Kingdom of God, or teaching on how to appoint elders etc. The whole concept of cross-cultural missions is a challenging one, in which we must walk with caution and humility.

'As a fellowship, we have had a training role in Asia since the late 1970s. We have teams that regularly go into that continent to train local believers. The Asians will then pass the benefits of that training onto their compatriots, while the teams come back and impact us with what they have experienced. It's a two-way thing. That's why every church should be involved in, and have a strategy for missions.'

Global plans

There are few areas of the world where Cornerstone is not in some way involved in outreach. For a number of years, a leadership programme has been in preparation aimed at releasing French-speaking missionaries into Europe. As a French speaker himself, it is especially dear to Tony's heart, though perhaps, one suspects, not quite as dear as his burden for Britain, and his adopted home of the Solent.

He is not of course alone in predicting that the 1990s will be a decade of fruitful evangelism and mission in Britain, or in calling for a rediscovery of the importance of prayer on the church's agenda. But it is in his assessment of the presentation of the gospel that he has something challenging – perhaps even prophetic – to say.

'Our task is to make the church evangelistic in a relevant way that touches the world around us. Proclamation evangelism is not what God has blessed over the last few years. It has a place, but it is not the strategy for today.

'I see a lot of similarities between the present house churches and the early Pentecostals. Initially they were just a group of people who were experiencing God in a fresh way, were enjoying him together and were regarded by others as inward-looking and bound up with themselves. Until, that is, evangelists were anointed and released from among them.

'We're reliving those days right now. I believe that lifestyle evangelism and social action will provide the backdrop for the evangelists that we need so badly. When they come forward, we are likely to see the answer to our prayers. It won't be the "superstars" of days gone by, but it will be through anointed men and women, who preach the gospel with signs and wonders following.

'These evangelists will function in the churches that receive them and with the backing of those churches, in towns and cities around the country. It won't be a "Pentecostal" mission, or an "Anglican" mission, but a working together for the fulfilment of God's purposes in that community.'

Large capacity

It is against the background of this co-operation and working together, that the concept of the city church has been mooted in certain areas of the country. The prospect of all Christians coming together as one large body in a town or city is not without its attractions. Is that perhaps what lies behind SCC's purchase of Southampton's Central Hall, a massive building with nearly 1,500 seats in its main hall? Tony's response is swift and unequivocal.

'We have no secret plan to take everyone over! Frankly I don't understand what is meant by a "city church". We are touching many parts of our city and have a vision for it, and since our new building is situated in the heart of the city, that must make us a city church. But there are other city churches in Southampton.

'The idea that John 17:21 will be fulfilled by all believers meeting together in one building to do things in the same way, is in my opinion naive and unrealistic. People aren't made like that. The truth is that competition sharpens our determination to do a better job, and that schism brings growth. What needs to happen, is for the believers and leaders in a city or town to stand together for the sake of the gospel.

'The Central Hall provides us with a big platform that in itself is a visible sign of God's Kingdom to the community. I feel certain that God does want certain churches to grow in size beyond what we have become used to in our land. I believe that by the end of the 1990s, there will be scores of such churches throughout Britain.'

*   *   *

Part of Tony's vision is that the building will enable the Cornerstone team to become a resource to other fellowships. The experience of many towns and cities is that large churches do change the shape of their smaller neighbours. Some years ago a prophecy was given in the church indicating that the fellowship would inherit a building for which their forefathers had laboured. Acting on that word, an attempt was made to buy every redundant church in the town, but without success. Eventually they gave up, and took on the familiar cell/congregation/celebration module. While this worked reasonably well, it become obvious to Tony in particular that the church was becoming regionalised. They were no longer one people, hearing one prophetic voice. Meeting together only about once a quarter, they were not experiencing God together and were therefore missing a vital aspect of church life.

Secret Enemy

The church applied to lease the Central Hall on several occasions, but to no avail. As Tony prayed about it, he felt strongly that they were being resisted by people who were anti-Christian. He therefore decided to employ an agent to work on their behalf. Within three days he had established that the Central Hall was indeed available to his anonymous client. By the time the council discovered who that client was, it was too late to say it was unavailable!

Southampton Community Church was now on the verge of owning a huge building with a main and minor hall, about sixteen offices and an apartment in a prime position – and all for £400,000. As yet the fellowship had no money; nor indeed did the members know anything about it. It's not the way that Tony likes to work; but on that occasion, secrecy was paramount.

Not surprisingly, the council soon started working

against the sale. They stated quite clearly that they didn't want a large church in the centre of the town. In their opinion Tony and his group ought to be out of town – and out of sight. In order to try and frustrate the sale, it was then decided to sell the building on the basis of closed bids. After prayer, the church felt to increase its bid to £520,000; on the day it beat the council by £20,000. A special offering immediately raised £100,000, enabling the deposit and professional fees to be covered.

The clear goal is to turn the building into a centre of excellence. And not just a preaching centre. Among other things, it is planned to use it as an arts facility, staging Christian productions, which will touch yet another sector of society with the gospel. Other possibilities include renting it out for music recitals or examinations and allowing various Christian businesses to occupy part of the centre. In that way, Tony confesses, he won't feel so bad about the mortgage!

Rich legacy

It is now almost a quarter of a century since Tony's dramatic conversion experience in Liverpool Cathedral. The benefits of that experience, particularly in the Southampton area, are undeniable. In addition to a strong local fellowship that reaches into every part of the city, a network of churches is making a powerful statement for Christ in the area. A time perhaps for Tony to reflect.

'House churches are, I believe, growing up into a new maturity. Yes, we made some mistakes, the kind that are almost inevitable in infancy. In majoring on the prophetic, and the immediate, we missed out on the rich Christian heritage that already existed in our land. A lack of theological training produced an imbalance among us, and we were for a long time guilty of ignoring social issues.

'But I sense, both in our own grouping, and in the house churches in general, a new determination to be relevant. The focus of house churches over the last twenty years has been to present the challenge of a love-filled community which is approachable by people round about, a community which expresses the presence of God in a fresh way. Hence the emphasis has been on fellowship, worship and relationship.

'All this has produced a very high level of commitment to each other. This has been expressed in various ways. On many occasions we have taken love offerings to cover the deposit on a house or the purchase of a car for someone in our fellowship.

'But equally, commitment means confrontation. We do not ignore problems of morality or lifestyle: they are challenged in the interests of reality. I'm not saying that such things don't happen in other churches, but they have been a feature of our approach to church life, and are only really possible where discipleship and relationship are high on the agenda. Perhaps this will prove to be our most enduring legacy to the body of Christ.'

Chapter 3

Terry Virgo: Missionary to
the south-east

Ask those evangelical leaders who know him to describe
Terry Virgo and the same kind of phrases crop up: 'laid-
back', 'friendly', 'unassuming', 'easy-going'. More than
once, he has been described as 'the acceptable face of
Restorationism'. It's a description that brings a smile to
his face – well, you wouldn't expect him to get angry!

But it would be a mistake to assume that Terry is less
radical, or more compromising than other house-church
leaders: nothing would be further from the truth. What
it does indicate however, is that Terry has been something of a bridgehead through which many evangelicals
have come to understand and appreciate the principles of
Restorationism in a fuller way.

He has never espoused the fierce anti-denominationalism that used to be a feature of some of his peers. As
a result, and alongside men like Roger Forster, he has
helped to ensure that the charismatic emphasis is now high
on the agenda of organisations such as the Evangelical
Alliance.

Until the age of 16, Christianity certainly wasn't very
high on Terry's agenda. Brought up in a non-Christian
home, his first contacts with the message of Christ were
like trying to find the proverbial needle. Unfortunately,
the haystack often got in the way!

Terry's parents sent him to Sunday school, as was fairly typical in those days. His introduction to Christianity therefore was a high Anglican church where he never heard the gospel. He later transferred to a low Presbyterian church where he never heard the gospel! However Terry sang in the choir until his voice broke, and then joined the church that had a table-tennis table.

He did however listen to the preaching; and for as long as he could remember he had always believed in Jesus. But he had never seen – or been taught – the implications of the gospel for his own life.

All change

Terry's older sister was at that time living and working in London. Like Terry, she had previously shown no real interest in Christianity, but when she returned home to Brighton one day, it was obvious to everyone that something remarkable had happened to her. She had in fact been converted to Christ through the ministry of All Souls Church, Langham Place. Like Andrew in Bible times she came home and 'found her brother'.

'She asked me point blank, "Are you interested?" Interested? I was fascinated! She was so obviously born again – whatever that meant – that I couldn't fail to be interested. At first I thought it was very presumptuous of her to say that her sins were forgiven and that she was going to heaven. But as she spoke of the resurrection of Jesus to new life, something started to stir within my own spirit. I got down on my knees and began to weep. When I got up, I knew that I too had become a new person. And I wondered why no one had ever bothered to tell me about this before.'

*   *   *

However when his sister returned to London, Terry was plunged into a period of spiritual turmoil. Sixteen years of age, and surrounded by ungodly friends, he lacked any real spiritual influence and friendship. He started to attend an Anglican church on the other side of Hove that had been recommended by the team of All Souls. Not only was it difficult to travel to, but Terry also found the formality of the services rather offputting. One Sunday as it poured down with rain, Terry toyed with the idea of visiting a large Baptist church nearby. He had often walked past and wondered what it was like. Finally he decided to find out.

'The moment I went through the door, I realised that these people had got what I had. Evidently Baptist people could be born again too! I felt something that I had never known in the churches where I had been brought up. So Holland Road Baptist Church became my spiritual home.'

Good shepherd

The pastor of the 600-strong congregation was E. G. Rudman. He was a godly man, and an excellent pastor, with a Bible-based ministry. He was also very evangelistic. Although there were not many public decisions in the services, every baptismal service would see people dedicating their lives to Christ. The church was also very missionary minded: dozens of people went out from there to serve the Lord in many parts of the world. Every spring there was a missionary week of meetings attended by hundreds of people. According to Terry it was impossible to belong to that fellowship and not be inspired and influenced by its vision for the world.

Mr Rudman exercised a great influence on Terry's life at a very formative stage. Although he was not a charismatic in the modern sense of that word, he was certainly a man of the Spirit. He often preached on the need to reach out for more in God, but it was handled in a Keswick sort of way, aimed at developing personal holiness and inner godliness. He himself had undergone a crisis in his early ministry after training at a liberal Bible college. It led to him spending a whole week before God giving his body limb by limb to the service of God. Not surprisingly, his ministry took off in a powerful way after that.

As so often happens, the church found it impossible to replace such a man. As a result, though still very evangelistic, it no longer has the great influence it once had. However, it has given birth to so much in the Kingdom of God, and was highly influential in Terry's life. When Terry wrote a book on restoring the church a few years ago, he dedicated it to Mr Rudman who was still alive at that time. It was an indication of both the esteem he felt for him personally, and the importance of his input into his life.

'It was also a statement of the links I feel between where I am now and where I have come from. As far as I am concerned, Restorationism is not a rejection of all that has gone before. It is a fallacy to see the "new" churches as in some way opposed to the "old". What I have come into over the last 25 years is a moving on from the roots that faithful men like E. G. Rudman, Denis Clarke and Campbell MacAlpine sowed into my life. Those roots consisted of a deep love for the word of God and a Bible-based ministry. Also I look back to Holland Road Baptist Church for the beginnings of my global vision. Any theology – Restorationist included – that departs from those roots will never prosper.'

Back to basics

That Restorationism has had its critics is both undeniable,

and unsurprising. However, accusations that the house churches are biblically 'thin' are on the whole unfair. What might not be unfair though, is to add that particularly in the early days, their emphases were somewhat hand picked. In the pursuit of God's prophetic truth, the so-called 'now words', the temptation was to relegate other areas of teaching to a secondary place. In the interests of liberty and freedom, the lines of Christian conduct and behaviour were redrawn. To some onlookers it was a breath of fresh air; to others, the thin end of the wedge.

Terry shares the classic house-church emphasis on living in the freedom which the grace of God brings to a Christian rather than under the burden of legalistic rules and the subsequent condemnation of failure. He cites the church at Corinth as an example: even when adultery was taking place Paul didn't use a legal stick as a means of dealing with it. He used an altogether different argument: 'Do you not know that your body is the temple of the Holy Spirit?' But you wouldn't hear Terry hitting out from the pulpit against the traditional teachings of outward holiness with which many Christians have been brought up. Rather, his approach is to work through the teachings of chapters such as Romans 7, and to seek to help people open up and shake off condemnation and heaviness. It's a method that is, at least in part, the result of his own experience as a young teenage Christian.

'My first four years of "abundant" life weren't very abundant. I lived an ungodly life all week and went to church on Sundays. I knew that something was missing from my Christian experience. One Sunday evening, the assistant pastor Alan Pringle preached on the text: "You did run well, who has hindered you?" Alan really nailed me to the wall with his preaching. It was a case of "Either live this life – or don't." That night I knew that I had come to a place of crisis. If I was going to be a Christian – and there was

no way I could turn my back on what I had experienced
– I would have to make a clean break from my associates
and habits. I knew deep down what I had to do. As it
happened, my friends dropped me as soon as they knew
that I no longer intended to go to parties and night clubs.

'So I just went to church, and stayed at home for
the rest of the week like a good Christian! It was all
horribly negative – and I hated it. Alan Pringle and his
wife befriended me and opened up their home to me. This
was a lifeline, because although it was a large church, most
of the young people were the children of the members.
It wasn't easy for an unchurched person like myself to
become accepted.'

Faith in deed

When Alan Pringle left, he introduced Terry to another
young man, Philip Vogel, who later became director of
British Youth for Christ. He was an evangelist and had
been given the responsibility of looking after a small group
of believers. Phil was also a very radical person. Although
married with a small child, he lived totally by faith, sharing
the gospel from door to door.

When Phil started up a Monday evening fellowship in
his home for people who wanted more intimate fellowship,
Terry got involved. The group met each week to pray for
revival and to study the Bible. One evening Phil said,
'Let's read through the book of Acts, and let's believe
every promise, and obey every commandment!' It didn't
take long to reach Acts chapter 2. Phil explained to those
present that he had received an experience of the Spirit,
but he couldn't put terminology to it, and he didn't have
the confidence to pray for anyone. In fact he didn't really
know nor could he explain exactly what had happened to
him, but he believed that there was another experience

of the Spirit following salvation. Terry recalled occasions when Mr Rudman used to preach on the text, 'Have you received the Spirit since you believed?' But again, it was never put in terms that would encourage people to seek the baptism in the Spirit.

One Saturday night, Terry rode into Brighton on his scooter. As the crowds milled around the seafront, he realised the hold that its night-life still had on him. It was as if, though truly born again, there was a part of his life that craved for fulfilment. Terry drove home with an aching heart. He threw himself onto his bedroom floor and cried out in desperation, 'Lord, if I am to go on with you, then you have got to give me more than I am experiencing at the Baptist church. I can't stand it – there must be more!'

Terry had met a Pentecostal believer who attended Peniel Chapel in London. Derek was happy, free – and he witnessed easily to people. He was everything that Terry himself wanted to be. The two friends used to meet up and go to Joe Lyons' cafe in London, where Derek would invariably witness to whoever they shared the table with. Terry used to envy his liberty, but hate the experience!

Avid reader

By this time, Terry was working in London. His three-hour daily commuter journey was an ideal opportunity for him to indulge his passion for reading Christian books, especially the biographies of the great missionaries. He also read about the baptism in the Spirit, but assumed that if John Stott and Martyn Lloyd Jones couldn't agree on the subject, he had better steer clear! One Sunday afternoon, strolling along the Brighton seafront, Terry watched a group of elderly Pentecostal ladies holding an open-air meeting. As some passing youths mocked the sound of their crackling voices, Terry was embarrassed at the feebleness of their efforts, but he also felt a deep sense of jealousy of their ability to witness for Christ. Within days, having come to the conclusion that he needed to be filled with the Spirit, he made arrangements to go and visit Derek Wilkes at Peniel Chapel. Thirty years later, the recollection of what happened to him remains etched on his mind.

'Howard Carter was preaching that day, but it was the local pastor who laid hands on me to receive the baptism. There and then I was overwhelmed by the power and presence of the Holy Spirit as I began to speak with tongues. I was so excited that I went to the back of the church and held my hand over my mouth. It was as if I couldn't stop. And I certainly didn't want to.

'When I arrived back in Brighton, my sister, who had led me into salvation, asked me to help her into the baptism. I had no idea how to counsel or pray for anyone in that area. As she knelt there, becoming increasingly desperate while nothing happened, I felt my joy draining away through my boots. For several days I went through a black experience as the devil challenged me concerning my own baptism in London. I knew that something real and dramatic had happened to me. The question was, whether it was only a temporary, passing encounter with the Holy Spirit.

'What eventually sealed the issue for me, was not the speaking with tongues, but the freedom to witness which I now had on the seafront and door-to-door with Phil Vogel. I had always been frightened of evangelism. Yet when I read the scripture, "Don't be drunk with wine: be filled with the Spirit", I remembered how my natural shyness used to be overcome by getting drunk with the lads. Being filled with the Spirit had a similar effect. The boldness and power that I now had to witness for Christ was nothing short of a miracle – and it nailed any lingering doubts about the validity of my experience.'

In the open

At first, Terry and Phil decided not to speak widely about the baptism. After all it was potentially a divisive issue. They began to pray that the Lord would bring it to a place of prominence at the right time. Within a few weeks, a group from the church went away for a weekend house party. During one afternoon which was scheduled for a walk, it poured down with rain. Mr Rudman suggested an extra session during which they would bounce questions off each other. Suddenly he stopped, turned to Terry and said, 'Something has happened to you during the last few weeks. Tell us about it.'

You could hear a pin drop as he shared his experience of the baptism with fifty or sixty young people. When he had finished, Mr Rudman turned to Terry. His pulse was racing as he waited for the reaction of this great man of God.

'You must bring all these young people into this,' he urged, 'and I'll come at the end of the queue!'

From that time, Terry began to lay hands on the young people. Many were filled with the Spirit and joined Phil and Terry on the seafront. He was given a great amount of freedom by Mr Rudman, who was happy to see people coming alive in God. Sadly a year or so later on, some difficulties arose regarding the baptism. As a result, Mr Rudman clamped down, fearing a divided church. Anything that had a charismatic slant was suppressed.

Full-time work

In 1963 Terry gave up his job in the civil service in order to pray for revival. For two years – the first with Phil Vogel – he prayed daily for an outpouring of God's Spirit in Brighton. While it would be another sixteen years before the birth of what is now the Church of Christ the King, it is clear that the roots of that work were planted during those days of seeking God in the mornings, and door-to-door visitation in the afternoons. It was a time of putting into practice the missionary principles of faith and dependency on God that he had avidly imbibed during those daily commuter journeys, and which he had so admired in Phil Vogel. When Terry entered London Bible College in 1966, it was very much with a sense of preparing himself to return to his native Sussex.

'I was one of the first charismatics to enter London Bible College. In the previous year, the college had for the first time allowed a Pentecostal student onto its campus. During my time there, I began fellowshipping at Richard Bolt's church in Buckingham Street. It was rough and raw, but a very exciting Spirit-filled church where the supernatural was much in evidence. After being exposed to the life and power of God in that church, I knew that I could not go back to the Baptist church. It was time for me to move on. I ought to add however, that on Sunday evenings, I used to go and hear Doctor Martyn Lloyd-Jones at Westminster Chapel. To this day, I have many of his books on my shelves. Westminster Chapel was so different from Buckingham Street, and the doctor to Richard Bolt; but it was an indication of where I was spiritually, and indeed still am. I want nothing that is outside the Bible, but equally I want everything that is within its pages.'

Small beginnings

When he left London Bible College, Terry was invited to lead a church in Seaford, a few miles along the coast from Brighton. It was a new fellowship, evangelical though not as yet charismatic. The agreement was however that Terry would be free to lead the church 'along a biblical route'. In practice that gave him a fairly free hand to do as he thought right, as long as he could provide a biblical basis. Within three to four years the fellowship was enjoying charismatic worship; and significantly, people began to attend the services from outside the local area. The foundations of Terry's apostolic ministry were about to be laid.

People who travelled to the meetings from other towns began to ask whether he would come to their communities. So Terry started travelling around, building up relationships with small groups of believers. Then a group of thirty-five people from a Baptist church in Brighton approached him, asking if they could get involved with Terry's group. They had experienced a real collision with their pastor. They said 'We're coming under your authority.' 'Well in that case,' Terry replied, 'my first word to you is to go back to the Baptist church!'

Reluctantly they agreed, and both they and Terry tried hard to reconcile their situation. He felt that in spite of what had happened, the pastor did in fact want to move on in God. In the midst of all this, Terry went off to the United States for a period of ministry. While he was in Sacramento, the Lord spoke to him, and told him clearly that it was time for him to go back into Brighton itself. When he returned home, the situation at the Baptist church was very tense. A few weeks later a small group that included Dave Fellingham was asked to leave an Anglican church over the charismatic issue.

Consequently Terry began holding meetings in a school in Brighton with a group of about forty people. In fact there were only thirty-six chairs, so latecomers had to make do with a child's chair! It was hardly ideal, but as it happened the pastor of Clarendon Church approached Terry within a matter of months, with a view to their group taking over his building. He had a small congregation, and a large dry-rot problem. The building was in a terrible condition throughout, but it became the base for the new work.

Prophetic times

The south coast of England has often been called Britain's 'Bible Belt'. Certainly, many Christian organisations and activities are based there, particularly in the area of publishing. It could also be argued that the beginnings of the Bible Week phenomenon lie there, specifically in the home of Denis Clarke. Alongside men like Campbell MacAlpine and the ubiquitous Arthur Wallis, Denis Clarke had a profound effect on Terry's spiritual development. He remembers Denis with obvious affection and respect.

'One New Year's Eve, Denis informed his wife that he was going to spend the holiday weekend alone with God in prayer and studying the Scriptures. He was apparently so blessed by this that the following year he invited a few friends to do the same with him. The year after that, a group of about thirty gathered over the New Year. I think it was the following year that I got involved. We just packed into Denis' lounge and spent equal time in prayer and Bible reading. It was breathtaking stuff. For several years it meant that I spent both the beginning and the end of the year in this way.

'Then one year Denis announced that Arthur and Campbell would be back from New Zealand in time to join us next year, so we moved to a conference centre in Worthing to hear these three giants of God. Many of the men who are now heading up significant ministries in this country were at those meetings. And of course, they were highly formative for me personally.

'Out of those beginnings came Capel Bible Week, and a host of other Christian events based on similar aims and goals. I don't think it's stretching things to say that Spring Harvest owes a great deal to those first Bible Weeks. And it all started when one man became so hungry for God that he set aside the celebration of New Year in order to earnestly seek God.

'Denis was a man of great vision and zeal for God. His emphasis on the inner life of the believer was somewhat similar to that of Campbell, who is a searching preacher of holiness. But it's probably fair to say, that neither saw the church in the way that Arthur did, as a related body of believers. It was probably for this reason that Arthur eventually became such a prophetic voice to the emerging house-church movement. Of course we need to emphasise the Holy Spirit's work in the lives of individual believers. After all, the church is not primarily about structure, but about people.

'But Arthur had come to believe that the emphasis had to swing away from an individualistic approach, to a church or body approach, in which those individual parts could grow and function as God had planned. I came to agree with him, that the recovery of the church was pivotal to the question of revival in Britain. After all it was the church that had turned off my friends, not the gospel. They had found it too dull and formal. I know there is a cost in following Christ, but I can't see that a boring church should be part of that cost! Gradually, the burden was growing up in me to see a church that could relate to my generation, and was flexible enough to contain the new outpouring of God's Spirit.'

Perhaps because of this changing emphasis, Terry began to feel slighty ill at ease with the Prayer and Bible Weeks. At a time of trade union power and strife, the prayer emphasis seemed to him to be becoming somewhat too political, with a consequent loss of anointing. So for several years, Terry plunged himself fully into the local

work on the south coast, enjoying charismatic worship
and ministering to other groups who invited him. But
the question still nagged him: How could the church of
the twentieth century recapture the anointing and success
of its first-century counterpart?

Back in touch

When an aquaintance casually mentioned that Arthur
Wallis was holding some meetings in London on the
recovery of the Ephesians 4 ministries – apostle, prophet,
evangelist, pastor, teacher – Terry decided to go along.
After all it was an opportunity to meet up once again with
a man he esteemed highly. He could hardly have expected
that his questions on the church would be answered, or
that he would find himself rubbing shoulders with men
who have since become household names in the British
house-church scene.

'As I listened to Dave Mansell talking about the ministry
of the prophet, I knew that I had found what I had
been looking for. I was immediately hooked. The fervent
worship was electric and very radical – so different from
the sweet songs of the Fountain Trust that I was used to.
  'I was introduced to other men, including Maurice Smith
and Barney Coombs. And I noticed a very young-looking,
rather spotty individual in a leather jacket. I wondered
what he was doing sitting among the leaders. After the
meeting he was invited to address the group concerning
the Festival of Light. He spoke so powerfully and with
great passion about the condition of the country and of
what God wanted to do. Now I knew why Gerald Coates
was sitting with the leaders! I immediately asked him to
come and preach in our church.'

*   *   *

It was around the same time that Terry first met Bryn Jones. Although he never became part of Bryn's Bradford-based team – according to Terry he was never asked to be – the relationship between the two men blossomed on the basis of a common vision to see the church restored to its New Testament pattern and power. Terry was a frequent visitor to Bryn's new-style Bible Week in the Yorkshire Dales, later becoming a much valued speaker and writer for *Restoration* magazine.

The early meetings of house-church leaders in Arthur Wallis' home in Devon have rightly been identified as a watershed for the new emerging movement. They were an attempt to draw together men of broadly similar ideas, and to provide an initial framework on which to proceed together. That they ultimately floundered is in no way to underestimate their importance. The meetings were initially conceived to discuss the thorny issues of Bible prophecy and eschatology (the study of the last things). However they developed both numerically and theologically. The clear recollection of those who were present is that God broke in upon them in a mighty way. Prayer and prophesying became the agenda together with a very real sense of unity and commitment.

Falling apart

The initial group of seven was soon increased to fourteen. Terry Virgo was invited to join the third wave which took the number up to about twenty. Having heard with great excitement the reports of the earlier meetings, he was delighted and thrilled at the prospect of joining the group. He confesses that what he found when he arrived was very disappointing.

'It was immediately clear that the brothers were not as

close together as I had heard. I could feel almost tangibly the tension between them, and after just two meetings the whole thing blew apart.

'The tension was mostly in the area of theology and ethics. Not surprisingly, strong men had strong convictions. For example, Arthur thought that John Noble was too anti-denominational in his views. *Fullness* magazine had run an issue entitled 'Forgive us our Denominations'. While Arthur himself was no supporter of denominational structures, he felt that John's attack was unnecessarily provocative and could lose us the fellowship and sympathy of other believers.

'There were also some very careless statements made concerning the Bible. Arthur was a very disciplined man, especially in the areas of prayer and Bible reading. He therefore had great difficulties with the views of those like George Tarleton who were quick to point out that New Testament Christians did not go around with big Bibles tucked under their arms. I too was very uneasy with an approach that seemed to mock the practice of daily Bible reading as some kind of legalistic tradition. I had listened to too many sermons by Martyn Lloyd-Jones and E. G. Rudman, and spent too many New Years with Denis Clarke to be taken in by such a notion!'

Under pressure

Inevitably, the man who felt most pressure in all this was Arthur Wallis. A world-renowned author and speaker, it seemed that he was being pushed in all directions, including by those outside the group who were beginning to look at the whole proceedings with incredulity. Feeling that he had to act in order to prevent the gatherings degenerating into chaos, Arthur drafted a letter which was sent to each of the brothers. In it, he came down on what he believed was the side of the Bible, and against the views that were particularly current among the London group of men, and which Arthur felt were unacceptable. Although a private letter, it was photocopied and circulated within days. The whole matter caused Arthur Wallis much grief, and to the end of his life he regretted using a letter for this purpose. However it is clear that Arthur was in a no-win situation. According to Terry Virgo, the letter merely served to highlight the divisions that were already apparent. With no middle ground left, he and the other men were left to choose between the two opposing sides. Although a sad one, the choice for Terry was not difficult.

'It was a heartbreaking time for me personally. I had only recently come on the scene, and now I was being asked to choose between perhaps Gerald Coates and Dave Mansell, or Arthur Wallis and Maurice Smith. I stood with Arthur partly because of the enormous respect that had grown up in me over the years for him. But most of all, I stood with him because I believed that he was essentially right.

'The question has been asked many times: did Arthur over-react? Did he listen too much to those who told him he was in danger of becoming a laughing stock? Or did he intervene just at the right time, and salvage something of what God was clearly trying to do at that time?

'I think that the brothers, like Gerald, took the view that Arthur was fearful of where things might lead if the grace teaching went too far. Gerald argues now that this would not have been the case, nor has it been so during the last twenty years.

'Only God knows the answers to all these questions. We have to take those decisions which we feel to be right in God at the time. In that sense, I don't regret the decision I made to link myself with the group that included Arthur and Bryn. But as the door of fellowship closed with the

London brothers, I couldn't help but feel that between us, we had scored an own goal.'

In spite of the polarisation that took place in Restoration circles at that time, the meetings had at least forced men of similar integrity but different convictions to think through the underlying issues of Restoration teaching. Even if the brothers couldn't agree together, they now all knew where they and the others stood. And there was no denying the validity of Restorationism itself.

Well versed

Ask any Restorationist what he or she stands for, and it won't be long before you're thumbing through your Bible looking up Ephesians chapter 4. It's difficult to argue with the charge that evangelicals have virtually ignored the gifts of apostles and prophets. Pentecostals have busily argued – and largely won – the case for the present-day use of charismatic gifts, while at the same time 'pastorising' most of their ministry gifts. Even those who have obvious evangelistic or teaching gifts have usually been referred to as 'pastor' – in the interest of avoiding the dreaded word 'reverend'! One is reminded of the quip by Bryn Jones on this subject: 'A pastor who has no sheep is not a pastor at all – he's just unemployed!'

But why has there been this opposition, or at best indifference, to recognising the gifts of apostle and prophet? Could it be that they are less easily regulated within a denominational structure? After all, where do you place an apostle in the pecking order of presidents, bishops, superintendents and committees?

Here lies surely one of the reasons for the traditional antipathy of house churches to denominational structures.

Although he chooses his words carefully on this subject, lest he give offence, Terry Virgo shares this basic
tenet of Restorationism, that denominations, however
well intended, are incompatible with the recovery of New
Testament Christianity that remains his goal.

'Restoring the church to what God wants it to be is bound
to be a radical operation. The surgeon's knife is never
painless, but where necessary it is life-saving. The church
has, over many years, even centuries, been accumulating
and developing human structures, which in many cases cut
across the word of God. It truly is astounding that so many
sincere, Bible-believing fellowships and Christians are so
loath to examine their church structures and practices in
the light of scripture. Things are swept under the carpet,
and obvious unbiblical practices are tolerated. God cannot
bless and prosper such fellowships in the way he would
want to.

'The five ministry gifts of Ephesians 4 have all too often
been interpreted away. I'm told that Martyn Lloyd Jones
did not believe in the ongoing ministry of the evangelist.
And it has been the pattern to call a man a prophet only
when he has died: Tozer is a prime example of that.
Perhaps we feel that we can only cope with an Isaiah or
a Jeremiah when they can no longer speak!'

Rising dust

'Once you are satisfied that it is biblically appropriate
to recognise apostles as those who plant churches and
also exercise a caring relationship with other fellowships,
you have to be prepared for the implications of that
recognition. An apostle or prophet does not sit on the
shelf gathering dust. Invariably they will create some.

'That is why we talked so much in the early days about

new wineskins. The relationship between a church and an apostle or prophet is bound to raise the question of authority. I don't mean this in a heavy sense. But if a church's authority or decision-making is invested in a board or committee, a church vote or the denominational headquarters, there are obvious areas of possible tension. But what has created the tension? Not the desire to become more biblical. Rather it is the unbiblical structure that feels itself threatened.

'House churches have sometimes been accused of being divisive. Those who make such accusations normally have a vested interest in maintaining the status quo. The truth is, that if you are looking for a glorious end-time church, you cannot avoid the radical process of preparation. This is bound to involve some demolition work. A better word might be "dismantling", because no one should go into a church situation intent on using a JCB! But don't forget that in preparing "the way for the Lord", John the Baptist had to make the paths straight, the mountains low, the rough ways smooth, and the valleys full. How dare we expect revival on the cheap!

'I was brought up in a church that was very dispensational in its teaching. Every year we had a convention when the emphasis would be on the end times. The overall theme was that the church in our day was going down the pan. Since we were now in the Laodicean age of lukewarmness and falling away prophesied in Revelation 3, there was little we could do except hold on. There was an inevitability about it all that was quite depressing.

'Significantly, the puritan reformers didn't believe that. They looked for the appearance not only of a glorified Jesus, but also of a glorious church that was growing, vibrant and successful. While there would be a diversity of opinions among house churches on this as on other subjects, we would all share the conviction that the end times will be characterised by a mighty outpouring of

God's Spirit upon his people, with a consequent dramatic effect on the world. So I'm looking for and working towards the preaching of the gospel in all the world.

'In short, the fulfilment of Isaiah chapter 2, "in the last days the mountain of the Lord's temple will be established as chief among the mountains; it will be raised above the hills, and all nations will stream to it." This is not to say that we will never experience hostility, or to negate traditional end-time teaching. The church in Acts was very successful, yet some were killed. In the same way, there will be conflict in our day. But in the midst of it all, I expect to be part of a worldwide dynamic people, not a pathetic remnant. That is the viewpoint that we would teach and hold in New Frontiers.'

Growing up

New Frontiers International – the name was changed from Coastlands when churches in Kent and the London area began to relate to Terry – consists of about 135 churches, half of which have been planted. The other half tend to be independent churches that have been drawn into the New Frontiers orbit. Growth in some of the planted churches has been spectacular: a church in Hastings now numbering about 500, began with just seven people. Similarly a fellowship which commenced in the home of Nigel Ring, now New Frontiers administrator, has since had to break down into separate congregations of over 100 each.

Friendships between Terry and other fellowships were already being built up before he came into contact with men such as Bryn Jones. But it was Bryn and those around him who helped Terry put the meat onto the skeleton of those emerging relationships. As so often happens, God used others to confirm to Terry the biblical nature of what was already developing between himself and other fellowships.

'I began helping various groups on the south coast and later I was invited into a church in London in an ongoing role. No one was using the word "apostle" in those days. I used to visit two days each month and spend time with the people and their leaders. Other churches in the London area then started opening their doors to me. When Arthur Wallis began to refer to "Terry's apostolic work", I initially resisted the idea. As far as I was concerned I was simply helping and advising those who came to me. Eventually I was convinced that perhaps such a ministry did indeed warrant the description, "apostolic" in New Testament terms.

'The important thing was not – and still is not – the question of titles, but the quality of relationship that has been built up between those fellowships and myself and the New Frontier team. The whole question of leaders and churches inviting input from other men is a thorny one. For some it is threatening and potentially divisive, and sadly there have been instances where that has been the outcome. But for many others the results have been liberating.

'The kind of apostolic relationship that I am talking about is built on the two pillars of friendship and gifting. Notice I didn't say "authority and submission". My experience has been that people will by and large receive your counsel and input only when they become secure and relaxed within a relationship. Not that I would want to ignore the question of authority. The churches and leaders that I relate to would not make any great structural changes without sharing it with us first. This they do by choice. After all, they want to succeed in God, not fail through ill-advised decisions. They see us as a point of reference. But just as an architect is not too concerned with a building's colour scheme, so I'm not involved in the day-to-day running of those churches. Firstly I haven't the time and secondly that isn't my function. One of the key elements that we try to set in place wherever we are invited is the principle of local leaders being allowed to lead. Democracy may be the world's best, but it is not God's best. Without a doubt the single most important aspect of church life is the setting in place of God-given leadership, coupled with a right attitude in the congregation towards those who lead. The actual structure of a church is secondary to that. I don't believe that any system must be rigidly adhered to.

'Critics of house churches have all too often homed in on authority and submission without any reference to its context. When removed from loving, trusting relationships, it is certainly dangerous. But within them there is safety and release. Relationships however must go hand in hand with gifting. Churches have approached us because they feel we can do something for them. There is no classic package that we bring to our related churches; every need and situation is different. But there are several important elements. First comes a teaching aspect, communicating the broad vision of where we feel things are going today in the church as a whole. Then there is the identifying of key factors within the local church which will either hinder or release that church into growth and blessing; these might include ingrained attitudes or structures. A third area might be to help a local fellowship to recognise emerging gifts of leadership within its ranks, particularly where a church has moved away from the church vote system.'

On the move

Historic links with men such as Bryn Jones and Arthur

Wallis meant that initially, the churches relating to Terry made the annual trek north to the Dales Bible Week. Not only was it an opportunity to meet up with the northern leaders, but also to receive and share in ministry. It was only a matter of time though until Dales became Downs, and Terry began to gather his own team around him. According to Terry, the inspiration for both of these developments was Bryn himself. With the only remaining link being a commitment to *Restoration* magazine, which itself was soon to come under scrutiny, the work in the south had come of age. The umbilical cord that had tied Terry to Bryn Jones and the Bradford group following the split of 1976 was about to be cut. The two men at present have little contact with one another. Terry's style is now much more akin to that of the London brothers, though having been arbitrarily bracketed in the former R1 group with Bryn and Tony Morton, he is not keen to be arbitrarily transferred to the so-called R2 group of Gerald Coates and others!

The truth is that today's house churches operate in less tight-knit groups than a decade ago; the result of a more mature attitude within, and a less hostile one without.

In one area however, Terry parts company with such as Roger Forster and Gerald Coates, though it's unlikely to affect the excellent relationships that have been re-established during recent years. It centres on the March for Jesus. Although many New Frontiers churches get involved with the annual event, Terry himself has removed his name from the MFJ council of reference.

'I have had some differences of opinion with Gerald and the folk behind March for Jesus concerning spiritual warfare. I'm happy to march – we have done so for several years – but I've become uneasy about the shift of emphasis towards cleaning up the heavens by marching, and chang-ing the spiritual atmosphere in our streets. Similarly I have difficulties with the notion of spirits over towns. I can't find it in the Bible. Having said that, I believe that God is in the March for Jesus project. I am happy to march and proclaim the name of Jesus to the community, but I am unhappy about marching to pray.'

In recent years, as some of those historic house-church links have declined, another name has been increasingly linked with Terry, that of American preacher John Wimber. New Frontiers, and in particular Nigel Ring were responsible for the administration of the early English conferences run by Wimber's Vineyard Organisation. At first it raised some eyebrows both inside and outside house-church circles. Wimber's teaching has not been without controversy, and he certainly wouldn't be called a Restorationist. Yet according to Terry, John Wimber is 'one of the most godly, generous men I have ever met'. And he is in no doubt that God planned their meeting together.

Laid back

Terry was in Cape Town, South Africa, when at the end of a meeting, someone came up to him and said, 'You ought to meet John Wimber. So much of what you have said is just like him. But you are clearer on the church, while he is clearer on signs and wonders. You ought to get together.' Terry's immediate reaction was that there was as much chance of him meeting Wimber as of meeting Korean leader Yongi Cho!

On the day before he was due to leave Cape Town, Terry suffered a slipped disc. This brother gave him literally armfuls of Wimber tapes to take home. Terry was on his back for nearly three months in agony, but with plenty of time to listen to tapes. As he did so, he began to warm towards a man who was big enough to talk about his own failures; and he felt happier with his theology of healing than that of anyone he had ever heard. As he lay listening to his tapes day by day, Terry longed to meet him.

Within days of his recovery, he had a phone call to say that John was in Britain and would like to meet him. Terry went to see him in a London hotel and the two men spent virtually the whole day together. Since then they have become bosom pals.

'John's ministry has been a real blessing in terms of our local church. We now expect to see more people healed than before. It has become a natural thing for people to pray for each other and we now have a healing team in our church. While we are not yet seeing as many healings as we would like, John's visits have changed our level of expectancy and the people's willingness to get involved. Perhaps John's greatest contribution is not as a healer but as a teacher and pastor. He helps people to understand that the healing ministry is for them, not just for the great evangelists.'

The Church of Christ the King (formerly Clarendon Church) now numbers about 800 committed members. On an average Sunday, over 1,000 people gather for the services. As the church has grown, it has had to adapt to changing situations. House churches are nothing if not individualistic. Yet as one plots the course of fellowships such as Christ the King and the Southampton Community Church, it is possible to detect certain growing trends (and the occasional growing pain!).

Almost all the larger house churches have at some time employed the structural model of cell–congregation–celebration. The first is normally a home-based meeting, consisting of up to a dozen people, and exists to promote friendship, pastoral care and possibly local outreach.

Congregations are somewhat larger, made up of several house groups and serve as regional sub-groups under appointed leaders. Since they are not too large, they enable the kind of open participation and intimacy favoured by house churches. They also serve as a valuable training ground for emerging leaders. In recent years however, a number of large churches have abandoned the congregation system, feeling that it lacks the impact and sometimes the quality of leadership that is required. The celebration on the other hand, is essentially platform led. In larger churches like Christ the King, they have tended to be monthly, and are a vital means of giving direction to the whole church, many of whom will not know each other.

New building

This was, broadly speaking, the system that Christ the King operated until four years ago. Then, partly as the result of a prophecy concerning the visible influence of a large church on such areas as the media, the decision was taken to bring the whole church together on Sundays in a large venue, while retaining both cells and congregations for mid-week activities. However, when the Odeon cinema announced that its hire charge to the church was to rise to £1,000 per week, Terry and the other leaders felt that such a use of the Lord's money could not be justified. A compromise arrangement of duplicate meetings at the Clarendon building was initiated. For Terry and his fellow elders, it was a frustrating situation. Somewhat reluctantly, they began to look around for suitable premises to buy.

Eventually they decided to put in a bid for a warehouse in the centre of Brighton that would meet their needs. Capable of seating up to 800 people, and strong enough to take the weight of an additional floor if required, it would be ideal for the Sunday morning celebrations. Smaller midweek activities would retain the 'house' values that are central to the concept of house church. After being told that their application for change of use would be rubber-stamped, the church's plan was unexpectedly turned down by the council. However, a subsequent appeal confirmed the scheme to turn the warehouse into a place of worship. The church now meets once on a Sunday and in home groups, but has disbanded its congregations.

'We teach the people that the celebration type meeting has a different value system from that of the cell. For example, if you went to watch a football match between say, Brighton and West Ham, it would be irrelevant that you didn't know everyone around you. After all, you are there for the occasion, to celebrate the event.

'To be honest, when we first began to grow, some of our people struggled with the notion that big can be beautiful. In our early days we taught them that the values of friendship and fellowship were central to everything we were doing. Consequently some tended to associate bigness with the kind of institutionalism out of which they had come. I once heard someone say – not, I might add, in our church – that the 700,000 people in Yongi Cho's Korean church, "wouldn't really know each other"! Of course they wouldn't – but what an impact a church like that would have in Britain. It would demand the attention of our nation and its media. Neither would the anonymity matter, as long as you built the more intimate values into other areas of fellowship life.

'We are now very committed to the concept of big churches. People stop and take notice of a large church, particularly in a nation of moribund churches. We are frequently given valuable media time simply because of our size, and therefore our perceived significance in the community.'

Men of like mind

Such sentiments might almost have come from the lips of Southampton's Tony Morton. Certainly the similarities between the development of the Brighton and Southampton churches are striking, including the vision to become a resource centre of excellence that can supply and train specialist ministries for other churches. Terry points to the New Testament churches of Jerusalem, Antioch and Ephesus as large, strategic Christian communities which sent gifted ministries into the surrounding areas.

A more significant similarity lies in the clarion call to evangelism that has begun to sweep through the house churches during recent years. Following a prophecy – 'just as I have put the church on your heart, I will put the nations on your heart' – Terry brought a word to the Downs Bible Week based on a verse from Isaiah; 'it is too small a thing for you to restore the house of Israel. I will make you a light unto the nations'.

Those outside the house-church scene might be concerned that so much credence is given at times to prophecy, in itself a fallible gift. According to Terry however, such gifts are only part of the process of finding God's will, often confirming what God has already been saying. The result has been a greater emphasis on evangelism within the New Frontiers orbit, with scores of young people giving a year of their lives to mission, and teams going out to plant new works. It was a time when Terry felt the Holy Spirit rapping him and his team over the knuckles.

'God showed us clearly that we were into the minutiae of Restoration. Should there be three or four tongues or prophecies in a meeting? Is the Ephesians 4 pastor a local or travelling ministry? We had forgotten that the outside world was dying without Christ. It was a clash of priorities and we were no longer in the centre of God's thinking. If we wanted to continue to flow in God's purposes, we had to make a major readjustment. In the last five years we have moved from three to over forty full-time evangelists within New Frontiers. These are men based in local churches but who can move around a region of five to six churches. An evangelist who stays put in one church will kill it, but in a group of churches he can move around stirring the believers into evangelism.'

Terry Virgo doesn't need reminding that the inherent danger of allowing the pendulum to swing in this way to a more outward-looking perspective, is that churches such as his may begin to lose their distinctive character and cutting edge. As house churches become more acceptable in mainstream evangelicalism they are becoming attractive to those who, in Terry's words, 'catch the euphoria, not the vision'. He admits that nowadays, some people link themselves with Christ the King who would not have done so a few years ago. For the first time he is facing the problems of people who want to join New Frontiers churches without knowing or sharing their values. While it is not yet a crisis, it is not difficult to conclude that house churches, or at least some of them, are experiencing a 'second generation syndrome' that ultimately affects all new groups. Only time will tell whether the first signs of the institutionalism that house churches so loathe, is creeping in at the edges.

Well spoken

'When we first started, the initial stigma surrounding us served to keep away any uncommitted people. But over the last five years, events such as Spring Harvest have not only exposed thousands of believers to the charismatic agenda, but have made that agenda less denominational.

As a result, when people move into our area, they tend to gravitate towards us, or at least give us the once-over. We do have commitment classes, a series of introductory lessons for people considering joining us, but with such large numbers going through, it's virtually impossible to get very close to people at that stage.

'I had a situation some time ago in which someone was arguing fairly heavily with me regarding the fulfilment of God's promises to the Jewish nation. It was immediately obvious that he simply did not understand our position regarding God's New Covenant with the church. Furthermore his attitude was very much that of the congregation ruling the pastor, who ought to keep the people happy at any cost; exactly the kind of unbiblical practice that we have sought to eradicate.

'But we are aware of these potential hazards. Indeed we had a prophecy telling us that if we looked after the roots, the Lord would take care of the fruits. It was a timely word reminding us not to neglect those foundational truths that are so intrinsic to us. It is easy for those of us who helped lay the foundation, to forget that each new generation must be exposed to those same principles. In that sense, the foundation needs constantly re-laying.

'But I am still believing for the revival that I used to pray for as a young Christian. And I believe that we have got to plant literally hundreds of churches throughout the country. Such a task is beyond New Frontiers alone. It will need all of us working side by side. Spring Harvest and March for Jesus cannot change the nature of our land. Only the church can do that, and then only when it is freed from its hindrances and unbiblical practices. Then we will see those large churches springing up which will in turn be a provocation to our generation to face up to spiritual realities. We have a big job to do.'

Chapter 4

Roger Forster: Keen fisherman

Perhaps the first thing that strikes you about Roger Forster is his accent. I am genuinely surprised when he tells me that he comes from south-east London, the community where he still lives and works. The diction is unmistakably BBC and care is taken to articulate each word correctly. It's an area in which the Cambridge educated leader of Ichthus Fellowship has worked hard, in order to be easily understood especially by interpreters abroad. The grey-haired, bearded man peering over his half-moon spectacles cuts an impressive figure. He is instantly likeable, self deprecating, and different.

Whether Roger Forster should be considered alongside names like Bryn Jones, Terry Virgo and Tony Morton is open to question. He certainly does not fit neatly into the main categories of house-church groups and leaders. He is by far the most open to the denominations; indeed he positively beams when discussing them, advocating that the church needs more rather than less! He stands in sharp contrast to the classic a-millennial stance adopted by most house-church leaders. And he wants to talk more about evangelising the unsaved than about healing the church – a most un-Restorationist agenda!

So what is the justification for Roger's inclusion in a book such as this? For a start, he doesn't belong to any mainline denomination although he is quite happy for

Ichthus to be called one, on the basis that any group
having a name is by definition a denomination. Also he
shares the Restorationist commitment to strong 'body'
growth, and has built Ichthus on many of the principles
espoused by house-church groups. And in common with
them, he exercises an apostolic-type planting and caring
ministry among related fellowships.

Having said that, Roger, and indeed Ichthus itself, is
highly individualistic. While backing off what might be
called Restorationist dogma, he has succeeded in building,
over the last twenty years, one of the largest churches in
Britain, comprising at the last count 2,100 adults and 700
children, meeting in over 100 neighbourhood groups and
twenty-eight local churches in London.

Perhaps the conclusions to be drawn from those statistics
are twofold: not all the 'house' or 'new' churches are
identical, and more important, Restorationism in itself is
not the last word in church growth.

Roger was converted to Christ at Cambridge, where he
was reading mathematics. Prior to that, the only Christian
influence on him had been one of liberal Methodism which
had at least produced in him an 'enquiring agnosticism'.

'I had read G. K. Chesterton's *Francis of Assisi*. Here was
a man who really knew God, and whom God had spoken
to through Jesus. I concluded that if God could speak to
Francis in the thirteenth century, there was no reason why
he shouldn't speak to me in the twentieth.

'Before going to Cambridge I had also started to read
the New Testament, albeit spasmodically, but during my
first term I began to read the scriptures every morning. At
Cambridge I met, for the first time in my life, committed
biblical Christians. Here were people who took the Bible
seriously. It was a shock to me because I thought they had
all died off in the Victorian age!

'I was taken along to an evangelical meeting, and there

I was exposed to the message of Jesus for the first time. It was so personal, and challenging: "If God has demonstrated his love for you by sending his Son to die for your sins, you have a duty to give yourself back to him." That's how I became a Christian. Looking back, I'm very thankful that I found the Lord during my first term. As a result I was able to get involved early on in the Christian Union and student mission. Also I'm glad that my first real Christian influence was one of mission. I had no doubts from day one that Christianity was a serious business with practical implications. Cambridge has a history of sending godly young men to the ends of the earth to serve the Lord. It was exciting to feel that I was following in that mould.'

In search of God

Roger began to feel a great hunger for God. He tried every church and Christian society that he could find, devouring the teaching of visitors such as John Stott to the Christian Union. He adopted a daily discipline of reading the scriptures each morning by the river. A daily prayer meeting served as another focal point for spiritual activity in his search to know and experience God in a greater way. For Roger it was a time of intensity that comes only rarely in a Christian's life. One day he was quietly reading a book that was criticising the Bible with a view to attacking it. As he read the words, 'Simon son of Jonas, do you love me?', he sensed that God was speaking to him through the words.

'It was as if God was saying, "Roger Forster, do you love me?" At first, like Peter, I couldn't answer. After all, I was just a scrap of dust in the universe. How could I say that I loved God? As I tried to mouth the words, the power of God came into the room. But it was more than just raw power: it was pure love, and it flooded the whole room enveloping me. I became immersed in God's presence.

'I opened my mouth and spoke out loud – but not in tongues. I didn't know that sort of thing existed, and I had never met any Pentecostals. So I just prayed and worshipped God out loud for three days while this experience lasted. God was so close, almost to the point where I could reach out and touch him.

'I didn't know how to interpret the experience, so I started to read the books of men like Paget Wilkes and Oswald Chambers. It was basically sanctification-by-faith material, very nourishing and unlike what I had been receiving in the CU. The emphasis was on a warmth of relationship with God, not a detached, formal approach, and on receiving a holiness that was God's, not yours.'

It wasn't until three years after his conversion that Roger spoke with tongues. His 'initial' evidence wasn't very 'initial'! However other evidences of the Holy Spirit's power in his life were more immediate. Gradually Roger found himself being changed from a standard CICCU member. His first lessons in living by faith happened during the summer when he undertook camp work and student ministry. It was an exciting time as God supplied his needs even to the extent of money appearing anonymously in his pigeon-hole. He began to think through other issues including the need for water baptism. Like most of his contemporaries Roger was seriously contemplating entering the Anglican ministry.

'But at that time it would have been impossible to do so while maintaining a belief in baptism by full immersion. I can see now that it was the Holy Spirit who was leading me into the truth, and in so doing, was making me different. I wouldn't like to say that the Holy Spirit never leads others into the Anglican ministry! But as the fullness of the Holy

Spirit became real in my life it raised issues of the kind that made it impossible for me personally.

'I might add that I didn't want to be different; nor did I realise that was what the Holy Spirit did to people. I'm a lot wiser now.'

Though that particular door closed to him, Her Majesty was soon to open another – two years national service in the RAF. Roger taught maths and radio to forces personnel, but quickly found himself launched into a ministry of evangelism that has remained close to his heart ever since.

'We saw what I can only describe as a mini-revival during those two years, as masses of airmen and apprentices came to Christ. About 160 Bibles were sold in just a few weeks. I've seen bigger things since, but it was quite remarkable for the 1950s.'

Love in action

The story of how Roger and his wife Faith opened up their home as a rescue shop to some of London's most dubious characters has become legendary in Christian circles. When a large Edwardian property in Erith came into the couple's hands they decided to use it as a practical demonstration of the love of God. It was typical of the 'hands on' approach to Christianity that Roger has always adopted. He admits that his wife has often been tested by her name, though she has always come through successfully! The tale is both compelling and cautionary.

'I have always enjoyed reading. I think it's good for a Christian to be as widely and well read as possible. I've never gone along with the notion that Christians have to be brain dead in order to serve the Lord well. Similarly, I don't think that it is particularly spiritual for a child of God to be only well versed in the scriptures. Of course the Bible holds the place of ultimate authority in our lives, but that doesn't mean to say that other books and writings are without inspiration.

'Faith and I felt led by the Lord into our rescue shop ministry. We didn't even have a honeymoon! But I had also been influenced by the writings of men such as Cripps on social democracy and Tolstoy on the status of possessions. I'm not embarrassed to say that I was challenged as a Western Christian by the concepts of communist writers, though not of course by their godless system and structures. We built bunk beds out of metal, and piled them high in our seven-bedroomed house. There was room for thirty-four beds and they were soon filled by some of the "hairiest" people you could imagine! Some came in off the streets, while others were brought to us by the friendly local police, who couldn't quite believe that we would take all their problems off their hands.

'We had lots of hurdles to overcome. We didn't even have a proper hot-water system to start off with. So we bought a hand immersion heater which we used to place into buckets so that our residents could wash in hot water. There were no carpets on the floors and we ourselves just slept on a mattress. By building benches around the bay windows downstairs, we made a meeting room for up to sixty people.

'Not surprisingly, we made lots of mistakes. Initially we took too many people for us to cope with properly. So we then restricted the numbers midweek, and were only full at weekends. During the week they went back to the psychiatric hospitals and the jails!

'We had no models to follow, simply a conviction that a central part of Christianity was to transform society by good works, and to demonstrate the love of God to society in a practical way. This was to become eventually one of the platforms on which we built Ichthus.

'Our period at Erith was invaluable as a trial run in working through these principles. It was another experience of living by faith. I had given away everything I possessed except a few clothes and books, believing that this was the best way to allow God to meet our needs. If he didn't want us in that ministry, I concluded, we would soon find out.

'God wonderfully supplied our needs at Erith, in spite of the mistakes we made. Looking back, I think that most of the important lessons I have learned in my life, have been learned through mistakes.

'Eventually Faith and I closed the ministry down, principally because we felt it was time to build a secure home for our young family. I wouldn't say that everybody ought to open their home as we did. We chose together to go down that pathway. However, all Christians ought to come to terms with the commission of Christ to "preach good news to the poor . . . recovery of sight for the blind . . . to release the oppressed".'

Back home

And so to Ichthus, and a return to Forest Hill, where Roger had been brought up. Situated between the depressed inner-city areas of Brixton and the affluent suburbs of Bromley, Forest Hill is fairly typical of an inner-city borough and urban sprawl that passes for much of south London. It is a community of needy housing estates and tower blocks where loneliness, fear, unemployment and deprivation stalk at every corner.

Roger and Faith moved to Forest Hill with a clear sense of God's leading, but uncertain of how that would work out in practical terms. For several years Roger undertook an itinerant ministry of evangelism and Bible teaching, including leading missions in universities and training students to work in evangelism. It was exciting and successful, but deep within Roger's heart a question nagged him. Why had the Lord directed him specifically back to Forest Hill, if it was to serve only as a base for his itinerant ministry and a home for his family?

In August 1974 the answer began to unfold. Roger was asked to lead a small group of Christians in Forest Hill whose common vision was to evangelise the housing estates in the vicinity. Together with Faith he prayed about it for a month before committing himself to the task. The group consisted of just fourteen adults and a few children. At their first formal meeting as a fellowship, the name Ichthus was adopted. It was intended to be merely a temporary term to tide the group over until premises could be found. After all, an ancient Greek word used as an acrostic title for the names of the second person of the Trinity, Jesus Christ, Son of God, Saviour, would surely never catch on in a fairly run-down area of London! It did however carry the meaning of the fish, thus presenting the new group with an instant logo. Twenty years later, the logo and name have survived the passage of time, not to mention a host of mis-spellings and mispronunciations. And the name of Ichthus has become synonymous with the church in the community. The premises never materialised, but the 'fish' began to swim.

The group determined to build the church on definite principles. The first aspect was that of fellowship. They agreed that their lives would be shared as much as possible with each other. So from the beginning they took great pains to build on the basis of love and commitment. They opened the scriptures together to explore the practical ways in which fellowship operated in the early church. They learned how to laugh and weep together; also the importance of unity and loyalty as expressions of the love of God in their lives.

Another important plank has been that of mission. From the beginning, they evangelised continuously. This has in turn led to a social action programme called 'Jesus Action'. If you are going to reach deep into your community for Christ, Roger argues, you cannot ignore issues like housing conditions, unemployment and social needs. After all, Jesus did lots of supernatural things like feeding the five thousand and raising the dead; but he also spent time with children, and washed feet.

Such activities are not merely humanistic: they reveal Jesus. On one occasion an elderly woman's house in the locality was flooded out. Ichthus workers cleared up and dried out the property. Some time afterwards, her grand-daughter knocked on Roger's door asking, 'Are you the people who helped my grandmother? I want to know more about this kind of Christianity.'

It's impossible to over-emphasise the importance of evangelism and mission at Ichthus. It undergirds every project undertaken by the fellowship, from a non-alcoholic pub in Deptford, to a confidential pregnancy counselling service in Upper Norwood. Equally, there is no doubt that the influence of Roger himself is deeply impregnated in the work. Though now helped by a team of eight other leaders, it is not difficult to see the development of Ichthus as the outflow of what has taken place within Roger over the last thirty years. As with all the major 'house' or 'new' churches, Ichthus bears the undeniable stamp of its leader. But then, nobody has ever denied that leadership is one of the strengths of house churches.

Into all the world

Roger Forster's commitment to hands-on evangelism pre-dates the current trend of house churches towards more concerted outreach. In addition to its indigenous work,

Ichthus has placed some of its best people into church planting situations in many countries including Istanbul, Nazareth, Cyprus, Cairo and France.

Alongside fellowship and mission the third plank of Ichthus is that of training. For Roger himself it is but a continuation of a commitment that began shortly after his conversion. If the church was ever to infiltrate the whole of society, he concluded, a whole army of trained, well-equipped and confident Christians would be needed.

But that would only become a reality if they were trained and taught, and the sooner that started in a Christian's life the better. Like most other new churches, Ichthus has a programme of initial teaching which new converts are encouraged to follow. Called 'Start Rite' the three-month course usually involves a small group learning together about their new-found faith: how to witness, how to receive the Holy Spirit, the importance of reading the Bible etc.

Once safely negotiated, Start Rite opens the door to a vast number of training programmes and activities, lasting from a few weeks to a year. The Ichthus Theology School runs for several weeks at a time, and members sign up for it. Other possibilities include FISH (Forward into Spiritual Health), now called Night School; and a training programme aimed at evangelising Muslims and other ethnic minorities called Network.

One thing is certain. The emphasis behind Ichthus' vast training programme is evangelism. Roger's commitment to that goal is summed up simply: 'Our aim is to produce confident and capable Christian workers. Along the way we also produce a few pastors. But we believe that a pastor must also be able to go out after lost sheep. Equally, an evangelist must be able to disciple new converts. After all, he is the first relationship that a new convert enters into.'

During its brief history, Ichthus has run courses both for in-house purposes, and for the benefit of the wider church of Jesus. For whatever Roger Forster is, he is certainly not exclusive or elitist. In fact he has some challenging but encouraging words for those churches who find themselves in the shadow of a 'mega church'.

'I have been told by those who have studied church growth in our area of London that it is to a large extent due to the influence of Ichthus that many other churches have come alive. It's a bit like the old dog who was on his last legs, so his owner bought a young pup to take over when he dropped. But the old dog didn't drop: in fact he's now running around like a two year old! I believe it can be, and often is exactly the same when a new church is established near an existing one. As long as you are there to evangelise the lost and not proselytise the found, you do change the spiritual atmosphere of a community, to the advantage of every church that is seeking to move forward in God. In this way, we have helped to stimulate other churches.

'I can truthfully say that we have never encouraged anyone to leave their existing church to join us, though some of course have done so. And on many occasions we have given our blessing and encouragement to converts and others who have felt that they would be better suited in another church. We have always worked hard to keep good relationships with other churches in any area we work in, and try to support inter-church activities where possible. If I may say so humbly, we have over the years poured a great deal of time and money into evangelistic and training programmes which have benefited churches and believers in our area, irrespective of denominational labels.'

It's a most un-Restorationist-like attitude. Not that Restorationists are confirmed sheep stealers. Indeed few churches of any description can avoid the temptation to encourage newcomers from any source. It's just that the Restorationist's agenda has been fairly self-contained.

Indifferent if not hostile to other denominations, they have tended to plough in isolation from other Christians. Not so Roger Forster. But does he really 'love denominations', especially at a time when many within them are asking serious questions about their value and biblical basis? A chuckle seems to suggest that it's not as simple as it sounds. Might it perhaps be aimed in the direction of one or two of his new church peers?

Only a name

'When I made the statement, "I love denominations", it was intended to be deliberately provocative on two levels. Firstly to shock those of the new churches who wanted to put as much distance between themselves and the denominations they had come out of. Secondly, it is a shot across the bows of the ecumenicalists, who are forever trying to join us all up, and who see our divisions as a sin.

'In my opinion, both perspectives are flawed. At its simplest, a denomination is only a name. That's what the word means. Once you have a name, be it Baptist, Assemblies of God, or Ichthus, you are a denomination. So relax, it's not painful, won't harm you, and need not hurt!

'But of course there is another side of the coin. When most of us refer to denominations, we mean the structures and organisation that lie behind the name. It is those structures that the anti-denominationalists have got in their sights. Unfortunately they are often afflicted with tunnel vision and fail to see that the structures are the scaffolding, not the church. The latter is in fact the life of the Holy Spirit, the body of Christ. At times the scaffolding undoubtedly gets in the way, and is clumsy. But you cannot reject wholesale the church on that account.

'You can of course reject or at least alter the scaffold. The structure is, after all, only of any worth as long as it serves the life of the body. Once it ceases to be a servant, nourishing and caring for the body, it must be jettisoned. Any organisational structure that becomes a lord, will slowly but surely start to control and ultimately destroy the life of the church.

'Some of the "new" churches and their leaders made a dogma, especially in the early days, out of rejecting all the scaffolding as moribund or at best stifling to the life of the body. I believed then and still believe now, that this was a sweeping and mistaken generalisation. It is just not true that all denominations are ruled by their constitutions and patterns. The last decade has shown that there is a great deal of body life outside the new churches. Also, it is not realistic. All life has to relate to and be lived out within man-made structures, even in new churches. Initially, like any new movement, the house churches majored on body life, but before long, patterns – even scaffolding – were formed. As long as they serve the life, they need not be feared.

'There are more than 22,000 denominations in the world. A few more won't matter. The dogma of anti-denominationalism is a more fearful thing, as is the dream of ecumenism. The latter will never work. Once you force two groups of people together, you can be certain that there will be some who will opt out and form a third group. A huge monolithic structure *called* the church, but not *actually* the church, would be hideous. As in medieval days, power concentrated in a few hands would soon corrupt. No, on the whole, I think that the Lord is not too concerned about the plethora of denominations; neither should we be. Nor should we be obsessive about trying to build a perfect church. Ichthus isn't perfect, neither are we looking to that end. When the Bible tells us there is nothing more perfect than love, it sets out God's priorities. We should never try to be wiser than him.'

Close friends

So where do Roger and Ichthus fit in with the other house-church groups? And how does he relate to the other men, in spite of obvious differences of theology and terminology? You would have to be ostrich-like never to have seen him in a photo with Gerald Coates. The two have often been pictured in the evangelical press leading a march or handing in a petition on the steps of 10 Downing Street. Although immensely different in many ways including background and age, they enjoy a close personal and working relationship. Gerald would also acknowledge Roger's influence in helping him develop his own theological views.

However Roger's involvement with men like Arthur Wallis, pre-dates that of Gerald and most of the other well-known house-church names. Both Arthur and Edgar Trout used to minister at weekend conferences in Roger's home in Erith. He was greatly influenced by such men as well as by others.

'The late 1950s and 1960s were days when Pentecostalism seemed somewhat dead in this country. Plenty of noise, but little power or progress. I used to join together with a lot of men, mostly evangelists, to pray for power and to study the scriptures. Arthur Wallis and David Lillie were our Brethren input, while Cecil Cousens brought a Pentecostal slant. The word "Restoration" wasn't used at all, even though our agenda included the recovery of primitive Christianity – but only from the point of view of being able to reach the nation for the Lord. After all, that is what the early Christians did; we needed and wanted what they had.

'I have fond memories of other godly men who influenced me greatly at that time. Austin Sparkes was a great teacher with immense insight into the scriptures. George Lang taught what the early Brethren men including Darby

and MacIntosh taught: that receiving the Holy Spirit was
distinct from the new birth. Most Brethren folk don't know
that! Edgar Trout was outstanding in moving in the Spirit
and operating spiritual gifts. Naturally we younger men
looked up to Arthur Wallis: his book *In the Day of thy
Power* was very much a handbook of the kind of revival
that we were seeking.

'Another brother who came to us was Willie Bur-
ton from the Congo. He was a gentle man, who left a
very real impression on me. He must have had terrific
power, to establish 1,600 churches. Anyone who thinks
that modern-day apostles are a recent phenomenon ought
to think again.'

Yet as Roger began to mingle with the men who were
to later become the pioneers of the house church scene
that was developing around Arthur Wallis, he began to
feel an increasing measure of disquiet. Above all, he was
uneasy with the emphasis on separatism, that seemed to
overlook the value and input of other churches. Any
emphasis on 'new' churches to the virtual exclusion of
the 'old' seemed to him both ignorant and arrogant.
In particular, he found the tendency to apply the term
'new wine' to the new churches, and 'old wineskins' to
the existing denominations as theologically insulting. The
man who had been brought to Christ via the testimony of
Francis of Assisi found the notion of narrow fellowship to
be stultifying. He wanted to hear from a variety of streams
within the church, and was looking for as broad a base of
fellowship as possible.

The second area of disquiet lay in the subject of discipleship: not in the necessity of it, for the need to train and
produce a better equipped church was not in question. It
was pivotal to the early house church conferences and
thinking. But as far as Roger was concerned, discipleship
had to be a means to evangelism, not a substitute for it.

Since those at the heart of the new movement had something of a crusading attitude towards what they believed to be a fresh revelation from the Holy Spirit, they were not particularly tolerant of waverers. As such, Roger found himself being moved away to the edges, because he couldn't go along with all that was being promoted.

Under the carpet

The straw that broke the camel's back however, was in the area of discipline, or rather the lack of it. If the two words 'discipleship', and 'discipline' shared the same root, Roger concluded, then surely there should be an equal priority given to the latter, and a consistent application of it.

'There were one or two instances in important matters, where people ought to have been disciplined. One was a moral situation, another was in the area of prophecy. During one conference, someone stood up and prophesied concerning a person who was dying, that he would in fact live. We found out shortly after that he was already dead when the brother prophesied! I simply suggested that we should make a public statement that we were wrong. I wasn't seeking to pillory anyone, but to demonstrate the importance of discipline in the exercise of spiritual gifts. These gifts were fairly new to most of us, and it was not surprising that we should make some mistakes. The real issue, as I saw it, was how we handled those mistakes. But no one would do anything, for fear of quenching the Spirit. That was in fact the very reason that I wanted a loving discipline to be exercised among us.

'As a result of those three things, my desire for broader fellowship, my priority of evangelism, and the issue of discipline, I found myself more and more on the perimeter of the emerging Restoration movement. It was something that Faith and I came to accept as being perhaps what God intended. We had appreciated all that we had received, but it was now time for us to move in a different direction.

'What I have just shared is my own perspective on those days and situations; others may of course see them differently. I would not want to say that my perspective is more correct or valuable than anybody else's.'

If the three founding principles of Ichthus were, and remain, fellowship, mission and training, a similar trilogy of characteristics has undergirded the church since its inception. Under Roger's leadership, the small group resolved by the grace of God that theirs would be a fellowship underpinned by love, humility and an openness to the Holy Spirit. Most of them had experienced church situations where back-biting, pride and sterile rituals had robbed the church of power and growth. They knew that unless they began their new venture in a specific and determined way, then Ichthus would never become a church that would salt its community in a powerful and effective way. The linchpin was to be that openness to the Holy Spirit. Though still learning in this area, the group saw the need to build flexibility into every aspect of Ichthus.

'We knew from the beginning, that especially in our community, we would need to be totally dependent on the power and working of the Holy Spirit. Without that, we were just a nondescript, distinctly ordinary group of irrelevant religious people. There have been countless times when we have been utterly dependent on the wisdom and insight of the Holy Spirit in a whole variety of situations. I have always emphasised the importance of the Holy Spirit in evangelism: he was not given to the church merely to bless us, but to equip us. Any 'charisma' that is not linked inextricably with world evangelisation falls short of God's intentions. The gifts of the Holy Spirit are tools for the streets, not toys for the body. In spite of all that God has given us since 1974, we know that what we have built at Ichthus would crumble tomorrow if the Holy Spirit was withdrawn from us. That's why we spend a great deal of time seeking to find the mind and will of the Spirit for our fellowship.'

This has been particularly important during the rapid growth of recent years. Limitations in the size of buildings and variations in the make-up of congregations have always conspired to produce something of an administrative nightmare. Seven years ago, the then 1,200-strong fellowship met in house groups on one Sunday morning and two Wednesday evenings each month, in congregations on three Sunday mornings, one Sunday evening, and one Wednesday evening; and together for celebrations on three Sunday evenings. On the fourth Sunday evening – you've guessed it – they met on a Saturday!

Little yet large

Unlike some of the new churches, Ichthus has not abandoned the house-group component. It is felt that particularly in a large fellowship, small neighbourhood groups are vital for the functioning of body life. It is there that discipling, sharing, laughing and crying take place as well as taking responsibility for the evangelistic work in the neighbourhood. So the fellowship still has a monthly meeting on Sunday mornings in homes which includes a meal together. In so doing it is making a statement about the fundamental importance of neighbourhood groups to the structure of Ichthus. They are not simply a midweek appendage for the keen folk!

The most obvious difference during recent years has been the growing importance of the congregations. It is here that believers break bread, and a family service type atmosphere pervades. Not surprisingly, the congregations vary enormously. For example you won't find many children in the Soho congregation, while others will be made up of largely older people or young marrieds. In one of the newer areas, Surrey Docks (or 'Quays' as it is now called!), the congregation is half white and half black. Such demographic differences produce wide variations in the character of the groups.

The congregations have responsibility for their own area. That means knowing their streets, and engaging in social and political action as well as in evangelism. The whole church now meets twice a month altogether, in what is called a 'plenary' or London Celebration. It's a platform-led celebration-type meeting. The absolute limit for any building that is available in south London is 1,400. By holding it in the evening, which excludes most of the children and elderly members who would find it difficult to travel, the church can manage to come together. It does mean that in effect only about half of the members are ever really together in one place, but such meetings are important for the vision that Roger wants to convey. And again, it reinforces the significance of the congregations.

This in turn has produced a degree of devolution. As a church grows, it is inevitable that the leader becomes less involved in, and aware of everything that is going on. Therefore, Roger has made delegation and the training of various levels of leadership a priority in ensuring continuing growth. At present he believes he has struck a happy balance between the measure of autonomy given to the area superintendent leaders, and the sense of mutual dependency that binds the church together.

Pulling together

Roger is unlikely however to find himself unemployed.
Although his apostolic team is somewhat less structured
than others, the leadership at Ichthus does serve not only
the twenty-eight congregations in south London, but also
some 120-plus linked churches. The relationships between
the team and those churches vary greatly. The church
in Norwich was the result of an Ichthus-trained worker
going to that city to plant a new church. As a result the
relationship remains very close. Others, like the linked
church in Yeovil come for advice and consultation when
they feel it necessary, and make use of the Ichthus training
programmes. Two members of that fellowship recently
trained for work in the Middle East. But as Roger is quick
to point out, he is happier with this looser kind of linking:
authoritative structures remain anathema to him.

'Our link churches are by no means clones of Ichthus, even
though many will have been influenced by our methods
and training programmes. There is no financial commitment to Ichthus whatsoever, nor any requirement that
churches think, operate or believe exactly as we do.
Some will have different views on, say, the ministry of
women. But as long as they share our vision of reaching
the unsaved, we are happy to link with them. Twice a year
the leaders all come together, and the link churches benefit
from conferences and other courses that we put on during
the year.

  'Part of the purpose of training others, is that in time
they may be able to take over from you. So in one sense
I look forward to the time when Ichthus will not need me.
Strange as it may seem, I can envisage the time when I
need Ichthus more than it needs me. By that I mean that
apostles, if one can use such a pretentious term, ought and
need to be rooted in a local church. Paul had a relationship

with the church at Antioch, to which he was connected and to which he returned. I could easily travel all around the world, accountable to no one but God. But this is not enough. We all need to be subject to the disciplines of those around us. Having said that, it is comforting to know that if I land in the Atlantic Ocean next week instead of the island of Jamaica, Ichthus will go on under the godly leadership of capable men.'

I wait for Roger to complete the sentence. I'm listening of course for the words, 'and women', and I'm genuinely surprised not to hear them. A faux pas perhaps? Or maybe the issue of female leadership is so much of a non-issue at Ichthus that Roger is using the word 'man' as an inclusive term, largely as the Bible does.

A woman's place?

The role and function of women in house churches varies enormously. Historically, the churches identifying with men such as Bryn Jones and Terry Virgo have emphasised the desirability of male leadership, both in the home and the church. It should be added however, that this has invariably been with a view to producing fulfilled not frustrated women. Head coverings have in some groups been used to symbolise female submission to male leadership.

It's a position that Roger Forster regards as somewhat sexist. If God has given definite and obvious gifts to a woman, he urges, the church should get behind her, not engage in a theological contest. It's a point of view undoubtedly reinforced by the ministry of his wife Faith alongside him. Faith is one of two women who serve on the nine-strong leadership team. Incidentally Ichthus prefers to use innocuous terms like 'leader', rather than more biblical titles such as 'elders' or 'apostles'. Could it be because the latter carry gender connotations in the Scriptures? Having said that, it is clear from Romans 16 that the female Phoebe held the previously male office of deacon (not deaconess!), or minister. More likely it is something of a reaction against the tendency in house-church circles – and indeed in most church circles – to use titles as symbols of power.

'I don't want to be called anything, and I particularly resist any ecclesiastical title. Clearly I am involved in apostolic work since I function in planting and helping others to plant new churches. But I'm not seeking recognition as an apostle. I do however have an insatiable desire for apostolic authority, but not as a tool to rule over people. I believe that the authority that Christ gives to the apostles and to the church is first and foremost an authority over the devil. I don't want authority over the saints: I want authority over Satan! Therefore I'm much more concerned with Paul the apostle than with the Apostle Paul. A man will be an apostle whether or not you call him by that name. Similarly, a man might be called an apostle but show little or no evidence of apostolic ministry. Apostleship is not a status or a title, it's a function within the body of Christ.

'It's the same with gender as far as I'm concerned. We have opened up every level of ministry and leadership to our women, including area and congregation leaders as well as house group leadership. Sue Mitchell, the wife of Roger one of our full-time men, is responsible for all our overseas activity. Not because she is Roger's wife, but because she has God's gifting in that area. In short she is the best man for the job! Faced with the question, "Is leadership male?" I would answer, "Leadership is leadership". If Miriam can lead in the Old Testament as well as anyone else, let's get behind her!

'It was this situation that confronted my wife Faith in the early days of Ichthus. From the beginning, she was totally involved with me, working alongside me and often taking a vast amount of the pressure and responsibility. Yet when we met together to discuss the work and to make vital decisions, she was omitted from the circle of men. Presumably it was thought that her wisdom and contribution was represented by me. Eventually we came to the conclusion that this was not right and that we had to be open to hear from both men and women.

'Theologically I do not even see the necessity for ulti-mate male leadership, which is a compromise put forward by some. However, I would want to qualify that in two ways. Firstly, it is probably the case that most people, though by no means all, feel more comfortable and relaxed with male leadership. Therefore there is a pragmatic rea-son why men will often be in positions of leadership.

'The other reason has to do with the social structures that exist among us. Whether right or wrong, society places a lot of demands upon women, particularly in the rearing of children. The role of motherhood during the early years of a child's life is crucial – probably more so than that of the father – and there can be no real substitute. This is bound to affect areas of ministry and leadership. What we must ensure is that where women do not have the kind of family responsibility that takes up much of their time, for example if they are single or without young dependants, we provide opportunities for God-given gifts to flourish, rather than adopting a closed position that robs us of the contribution of our women folk. The issue is not male or female; it is how we can co-operate together in order to provide the church with the best that we have between us.'

Heavenly armour

Although Ichthus has never owned a hall or meeting-place of its own, the fellowship did some years ago purchase

a large Edwardian house in Forest Hill as its administrative and training base. Later the adjoining house
became available and this has now been converted into
a prayer house for both individual and corporate use.
Indeed prayer and spiritual warfare have taken on an
increasing importance during recent years as the church
has confronted local issues in the name of Christ. Though
not everyone agrees with him in this area, Roger is firmly
convinced that the forces of darkness have to be recognised
and fought on a wider level than most Christians are ready
to acknowledge.

'We have moved deeper during recent years into prayer
and spiritual warfare. It's not only that we are praying
more; rather we are emphasising more strongly than
before the concept of doing battle with the forces of
wickedness, and engaging and pulling down territorial
spirits that rule over certain areas and peoples. For example we had a very interesting prayer meeting in which we
acted out the fall of the spiritual powers over Turkey. A
week later we received permission to begin evangelism
in a shopping mall in that country. Similarly with Nepal:
when Roger Mitchell went out there shortly afterwards,
the doors opened wide to us.'

As so often happens it was through a personal crisis not
a theological discovery that the importance of spiritual
warfare was born in Roger and Faith. The church had
been in existence for about eight years when the couple's
oldest child Chris was diagnosed as suffering from a rapidly
growing leukaemic-type cancer. It came at a time when
threats and curses had been addressed to the church and
to Roger particularly.

   The prognosis was very poor: Chris was given just twelve
weeks to live. Totally devastated, the family turned to the
fellowship for support. An army of prayer warriors was

mobilised as the church began to fast and pray against what they perceived to be a satanic onslaught.

Prayer of faith

Roger and Faith were put in touch with an American brother who had been used of the Lord in a healing ministry. While the church prayed and fasted, he agreed to visit the hospital with them to pray for their son. The results were dramatic. By the next day all his symptoms had vanished and to this day no further cancer cells have been discovered. He now lives the normal life of someone in his late 20s and has given Roger and Faith a grandson. Through a situation that came right into their own home, they learned a practical lesson about the power of prayer, the meaning of love, and the importance of unity.

Prayer and praise marches throughout south London have been a feature of Ichthus' outreach for many years. When Graham Kendrick joined the church in the mid-1980s he developed a more aggressive style of music that was to ultimately give birth to the March for Jesus initiative. At first the Make Way marches were primarily local church events. Notable among those was the 300-strong march through Soho, following which the police raided and closed down many of the places of ill repute. The first Make Way record was in fact recorded one Saturday evening in a school hall following an Ichthus march in Lewisham in the afternoon. It soon became clear however, that not only were the marches successful but that the church was merely scratching the surface with regards to their potential. When an Ichthus member who worked in Smithfields meat market was given permission to use the market free of charge, Roger and the other leaders were unsure of how best to use the facility. Perhaps a concert, or an exhibition, or maybe stalls selling Christian goods?

Roger consulted Lynn Green at Youth With A Mission and Gerald Coates, and they came to the conclusion that a march through the city would be the best answer. Initially they wanted to start at the Tower of London and then go round the city walls, but eventually had to confine themselves to what the police would allow. To their amazement the whole concept began to gather a huge momentum: on the day, 15,000 people turned up to pray and praise.

Things have snowballed enormously since then to the extent that March for Jesus is now an international project using mostly material that Graham has specially written for the occasion.

Church on the move

'March for Jesus is first and foremost a mobile prayer and praise meeting. For many of us – though by no means for everyone – there are also connotations of spiritual warfare. We believe that we are engaging spiritual powers and cleansing the spiritual atmosphere as we proceed.

'Many of the buildings in our towns and cities are symbols of power and authority. Behind them lie supernatural powers. The stock market collapse shortly after our march was an indication to some of us that we were affecting the supernatural powers in the City of London. But many people march not aware that such could or should happen, but only to praise Jesus together on the streets. Another aspect of marching is the opportunity it provides for a visible display of unity. Many Christian groups feel able to join in, including Catholic believers in Jesus. As such, marches serve as a testimony to the world as well as to the heavens. Many Christians have written to us saying that they have met other believers from their own town whom they didn't even know existed! As a result, many ongoing relationships have been forged through marching together.'

With such a positive attitude towards cleansing the heavens and engaging in spiritual warfare through such activities as prayer and marching, you might expect Roger to adopt the fairly standard Restorationist view of eschatology. But here again he is something of an exception. Like Arthur Wallis, but unlike most of his peers, Roger remains committed to pre-millennialism. He reacts immediately and positively when asked whether he expects Christ's return at any time, rather than according to the Restorationist time scale. While he stops short of advocating a literal one-thousand-year reign of Jesus on earth, he rejects the notion, perhaps less widely held now in Restoration circles, that the church will usher in the time of peace on earth by subduing spiritual and earthly authorities before Christ's return.

'In the early days, there was an immaturity that almost contrived to throw out the second coming of Jesus. In fact the way that some people spoke, there didn't seem much for Jesus to come back for! It tended towards the Latter Rain heresy, which taught that God's sons would be given immortal bodies before the return of Christ to the earth.

'It is perfectly proper in my view to teach the doctrine of "Kingdom Now". The Kingdom of God has indeed arrived on earth in Jesus. It lives through our hearts and lives, and we are to do our utmost to extend the influence of that rule or Kingdom. But it is not for us to say how much of the Kingdom of God we can have now. The only answer must be, "as much as possible!" However there is a part that God has reserved for himself – "Vengeance is mine, I will repay" – and that will take place at the judgement seat of Christ. At present he is holding back those judgements because we are in a Kingdom of grace.'

Throwaway world?

'I'm staunchly pre-millennialist; God didn't create the earth
to simply screw it up like a piece of paper and throw it
away. His plan is to redeem it in Christ and to demonstrate
this redemption as it is reigned over by Jesus himself. You
can't find many scriptures about going to heaven when you
die, but you can find plenty about reigning in a new heaven
and a new earth with Christ. I don't know whether this will
be a literal period of 1,000 years. It's impossible to say
since the book of Revelation is so full of metaphors. But
we will have a job to do, assisting Christ in the subduing
of the earth to the will of the Father. It will be a limited
expression of the potential of God in creation.

'I believe that most of the rewards hinted at in the
New Testament refer to the millennium. Furthermore the
scriptures seem to point to the fact that not all Christians
will reign with Christ; Paul says that we are "heirs of God;
but joint heirs with Christ if we endure with him". To
be in that regenerated earth requires faithfulness and
persistence. The millennial period will be one of reigning
then after training now. For that reason we should not
be indifferent to the idea of rewards. They are to be a
stimulation to holiness and Christian service.'

Role model

Few would doubt that the growth of Ichthus during the last
two decades has been one of the great success stories of
British Christianity in the twentieth century. The church
and its leader seem to have earned widespread respect
even in non-charismatic circles. The fact that Ichthus is
larger than any other Restoration church may in itself be
significant. While Roger retains a respect and affection
for the pioneers of the house-church movement, it is clear

that he now feels more comfortable in the wider body of evangelicals. He is unlikely to change that stance.

'I think that the house-church movement has served the purposes of God as a pioneering, stimulating guerilla movement. As such it was meant to spill back its blessings into the church in the next generation. By and large that has happened. Many things that the house churches stood for and were criticised for in the early days, have now been taken up by the wider church. It is similar to the experience of Pentecostal believers early in this century. The revelation they received concerning the gifts of the Spirit was eventually taken on board by those who said that speaking in tongues was of the devil! Had that revelation remained in the Pentecostal denominations, then we would not have been as far down the road as we are today.

'But I think it was probably of God that the house-church movement broke up as it did: there was a pretentiousness creeping in which was not helpful. The fact that most of us are still seeking to move on together is due in great part to Gerald's care and prayer which have led to people getting together again, though on a much more open basis.

'Almost inevitably, the house-church movement has become more mature with the years. That is good, as long as maturity does not lead to respectability. A respectable church will never be able to evangelise this nation. So we need to go on saying those things that are no longer rejected by the wider body of Christ. After all, the reason we said them in the first place, was that others might jump on the bandwagon!'

Chapter 5

Gerald Coates: Scourge of the status quo

'Your son won't survive the night. You may as well go home'. The unconscious frame of the 17-year-old accident victim lay broken in many places. It seemed as if another statistic was about to be added to the list of motor cycle fatalities. The brief life of Gerald Coates would be remembered and recorded on the granite of a tombstone.

But in the providence of God, Gerald survived. Though he would remain unconscious for a week, and in hospital for nine weeks, Gerald was to make a marvellous recovery. The blood clots around his brain dissolved, his eyesight was restored, and the many broken bones began to knit together.

Thirty years later it would be hard to imagine the British evangelical scene without Gerald Coates. Controversial he certainly has been; perhaps there is some truth in the suggestion that he has at times deliberately courted it. Maybe, as the *Sunday Times* remarked, there is something of the showman in his personality and approach. But against that, it has to be said that Gerald is one of the warmest, most generous people around: colourful, yet inspiring. He is instantly likeable, thoroughly charming. And when he speaks, you want to listen. Such is surely the hallmark of a prophet.

Very few evangelicals have exercised the kind of influence or shaped the development of church life during the last quarter of this century in the way that Gerald has. Still not yet 50, he has been centre stage for as long as most can remember: a far cry from a fairly uneventful childhood.

Early days

'I was born in Woking, Surrey, about five miles from Cobham. My mother was a nominal Anglican, my father probably less than a nominal Anglican! Together with my younger brother and sister, we grew up in Stoke D'Abernon, a small village outside Cobham. My only real claims to fame during my early years were that I failed my 11-plus spectacularly, and rubbed shoulders at school with Marc Bolan, who was later to achieve stardom as a pop singer.

'Between the ages of 5 and 11, I had gone along to the local Anglican Sunday school which was run by a very godly man. Like most congregations, it was made up of some who were genuine believers, and others who were just religious; not that I knew the difference at the time.

'At the age of 11, I was invited to go to the Bible Class. It was in a different location, and was run by different people. I decided to part company with the Anglicans, a decision for which they have since been profoundly grateful!'

Gerald was invited by his cousin to a youth camp in Coombe Bissett near Salisbury, where he heard the gospel of Jesus Christ clearly presented for the first time. Believing what he heard to be true, he made a response, gave his life to Christ, and there began what he now refers to as the 'six unhappiest years of my life'.

*　　*　　*

'You find out a lot about yourself between the ages of 11 and 18. Most of what I found out I didn't like. I used to walk two miles on a Friday evening to a Bible Club with my next-door neighbour. I just knew that if it was possible to know God like these people knew him, then I ought to hang around with them. But as a 17-year-old, my Christian life was going nowhere. Year after year I made my annual pilgrimage to youth camp where I would once again re-dedicate my life to the Lord, but without any real lasting effect. I was living in a twilight zone – too wordly to be any good to God, yet too religious to be any good to the world. I was deeply unhappy.'

Called to serve

And so to the accident. During the many weeks of rehabilitation, Gerald not surprisingly went through a process of deep self-examination. What if his life had been snuffed out like a candle? How would he have explained his promiscuous behaviour to a holy God? Slowly he began to feel that his life had been preserved for a purpose, and that God's hand was upon him for a specific task. It was the motivation he needed to clean up his private life and flee the misery of the twilight zone.

As soon as possible following the accident, Gerald began to attend the only evangelical fellowship in Cobham, the Plymouth Brethren. In a manner reminiscent of Pharaoh's dream in the Old Testament, his six years of unhappiness were replaced by six years of almost unbridled enjoyment with the Brethren. Most important, the unlikely setting of the PBs became the place in which Gerald began to work through various theological and structural issues that would become the foundation of his future ministry.

'I learned a great deal from the Brethren despite their

strong line on the kind of dispensationalism which ruled out apostles and prophets, signs and wonders and the gifts of the Spirit. On a Sunday morning we used to go through a fairly grim breaking of bread service, followed by a happy time after the meeting where people enjoyed themselves with each other. I could never work out why we didn't have tea and biscuits as well, and make a thoroughly good job of it. It would of course have created a corporate heart attack even to have suggested it!

'Eventually there was a split in the fellowship. We were at Filey at the time, and when we returned home we found that twenty had left and twenty had stayed. I couldn't tell you even now what the issues were, but I was taken by the fact that the twenty who left were more gracious than those who stayed – so I went with them!'

Closed door

After three years, the second group decided to go back and rejoin the Brethren fellowship. For Gerald and his wife Anona however, the route back to the Brethren fold was to all intents and purposes no longer open. Something life-changing had happened to Gerald on a bicycle – no, don't worry, this time he broke the mould, not his head! Cycling one day through Cobham on his Royal Mail issue bike, he began to sing the hymn, 'Love Divine'. As he reached the phrase, 'changed from glory into glory', the words came out as 'keyarunda sadavoostoo' (Gerald's spelling not mine!). Uncertain as to what had taken place, Gerald shared the experience with a friend who helped him enter into the fullness of the Holy Spirit. It was inconceivable that Gerald could now subsume his experience in order to re-enter the Brethren assembly.

So twenty-four years ago, with his wife Anona and three friends, what became the Cobham Christian Fellowship was born in the couple's front room. Devoid of role models, it was to pass through many learning stages, starting from day one. Within a short time however, the familiar though not imitated features of house-church life began to emerge.

'As I waited nervously on the first Sunday for our friends to arrive, I looked around the front room to see if everything was in order. Everything was perfectly in order – and it suddenly horrified me. In the centre of the room the coffee table was covered with a white cloth, on which stood a glass of Ribena and a plate of bread, totally dominating the proceedings. Before anyone had arrived, I had unwittingly created an atmosphere of religion rather than one of fellowship, in which the breaking of bread should find its true context. My first discovery was that although I had left the Plymouth Brethren, not all that was of the PBs had left me. I quickly put the coffee table away, and perched the bread and Ribena on the television set until needed!'

Real friends

In the relaxed and informal atmosphere that ensued, the agenda of the new fellowship became established. Not surprisingly the stages that the small group passed through read very much like a house-church manual. First and foremost – and this will come as no surprise to those who know Gerald – the group determined to root out all religious pretentiousness, and replace it with a sense of reality and true friendship. This involved eating and drinking together as well as a practical dimension of love that included both emotional and financial care.

Friendship is a word that crops up often in Gerald's vocabulary. He is clearly more comfortable with it than

the word 'fellowship'. One suspects that the latter has too
many religious connotations for him. Friendship still lies
at the heart of the church, now named Pioneer People and
covering a wider area. Over the years many members have
made their homes in Cobham itself in order to be within
walking distance of their Christian brothers and sisters.
This in spite of the obvious difficulties of finding suitable
housing in a small town community, for whose inhabitants
commuting is a way of life.

Within the sense of security that friendship inspires,
commitment one towards another became a welcome
by-product. Then came the recognition of gift and ministry, and most important leadership. It was, and still
is, the familiar house-church formula that continues to
challenge denominational Christianity with its emphasis
on relationship and body life. In the fellowship's early
stages, such a radical agenda was very attractive to those
who didn't fit in anywhere else, or who were looking for
an alternative to a more organised, institutional religion.
Many 'dismembered parts' (Gerald's words!) were added
to the group. Nearly a quarter of a century later, the
church now numbers in excess of 700.

All change

In 1991 the Cobham church changed its name to Pioneer
People. This coincided with the 'Event in a Tent', an
evangelistic celebration of twenty-one years of Kingdom
building in the town, with the aim of taking the gospel
into every home in Cobham. But according to Gerald, it
was more than a change of name.

'The decision to change CCF to Pioneer People was a
conscious one. With all that is now going on in our area
outside of Cobham, we felt it was time we called ourselves

something that did not limit us geographically. The word Pioneer also conveys something of the sense of apostolic calling and vision that we feel. Like so many of the new or house churches, we had to give ourselves in the early days to the task of building a local fellowship along definite lines and principles. After all we would have lacked any credibility at all, if we had simply made high-sounding noises about the Kingdom and the church. We had to prove over a period of time that what we were doing was of God and that it could work and stand the test of time. We had no role models when we started; therefore our first task was to create some.

'That phase is now largely complete. There is still much to be done in Cobham and the surrounding towns, and to that end we have a local team that is engaged in church planting, training leaders and overseeing a number of projects in the area. Then I have a national team whose members are involved in church planting countrywide, servicing initiatives ranging from help to the suffering church to our AIDS project ACET, and serving the network of eighty churches that have linked in to Pioneer.

'Most of the people who belonged to Cobham in the early days, lived within walking distance of each other. But we have never encouraged a preaching centre mentality: indeed, we have sent out many excellent people who have become the backbone of churches in Farnham, Molesey, inner-city Tooting and Wandsworth. It is no exaggeration to say that at least 1,000 people have come from the initial group of five that began meeting in 41 Tarter Road.'

Reaching out

Gerald Coates is a gregarious sort of person. He clearly

enjoys close contact with other people. When the house-church leaders separated acrimoniously in the late 1970s, it was Gerald who sought, and has continued to seek, to rebuild relationships, albeit on a different level. He particularly seems to thrive when surrounded by ministers and leaders in a seminar situation. Many have come away from such occasions deeply affected, feeling that Gerald has put his finger on the real issues that are to the forefront of the church today. Perhaps, as Terry Virgo has commented, Gerald has majored on shooting down, often with great humour, the Aunt Sallies that raise their heads in church life (including house-church life!). However, one is invariably left thinking that he has addressed with prophetic insight and incisiveness, the areas that are nearest to God's heart in our day.

En route

But although a pioneer, Gerald is quick to recognise the influence of those believers who have helped and shaped him at various stages of his life. In his early days, he recalls, they were the unknown, unsung believers of the Brethren assembly. The irony of Gerald's pun about 'getting all the Brethren out of me,' is not lost on him.

'You do learn from other people who are able to take you one step further onto the next stage of the journey. It is important to recognise this in our lives as Christians. It stops us becoming arrogant and proud when we realise that God has used other brothers and sisters to bring us to where we now are. One of the mistakes that the house churches made during their early immature days, was to turn our backs on our past. The fact that others may not be coming with us on the next stage of our journey, is no reason to reject or cease to respect them; after all, we might not have been where we are today without their help.

'I like to think that my life and ministry today are bearing the fruit of the seeds of integrity, love and care that were sown in me by men and women in the Brethren assembly. No doubt they were not aware at that time of what they were doing. I'm a great believer in hanging around people who are fruitful. After all the seeds of the fruit are in the fruit itself, not in the tree. So if you eat of the fruit of people's lives, you will eventually digest some seeds which in turn will begin to produce fruit in you. What a wonderful, exciting principle!

'The writings of A. W. Tozer and Watchman Nee influenced me greatly during my 20s. I think you would probably find that the same was true of most house-church leaders in the early days. Nee's call for a whole new level of spirituality and Tozer's plea for a return to New Testament Christianity struck a chord in many of our hearts.

'Having said that, I wouldn't now encourage any of my young guys to read A. W. Tozer, but that is because of where we are at today, twenty-one years later. He had a number of views on various issues that I would not hold today, but that simply proves what I have just been saying. People tend to influence us only to the next stage of our experience, not the next two stages; we have to look to others for that. The fact remains however that Tozer's seeds in me have been influential in my input into the lives of others, but only as those seeds have become part of a much wider thing that God has done in my life over the years.'

Wise words

Not surprisingly, the main influences on Gerald during

the last twenty years have been from within the 'new church' movement. Maurice Smith was one of the earliest. The two names that slip most readily from Gerald's lips however, are those of John Noble and Roger Forster. In the former, Gerald found someone whose wisdom he particularly appreciated, coupled with an ability to see the other person's point of view. Gerald is equally warm in his praise of Roger.

'I am an intuitive sort of person: that tends to be a characteristic of the prophetic gift. Roger has the kind of theological background that has often provided me with something on which to hang my prophetic spirit. His utter rejection of Calvinism, and strong emphasis on the human response to a God who is looking for people through whom his will can be done, has been particularly helpful.'

Relationships between leaders in the London area inevitably grew closer following the well-publicised split among the house-church leaders in 1978. As one of the youngest members of the original group of fourteen, Gerald might easily have been affected more deeply than others, but if he was, it doesn't show. He chuckles – perhaps a little too convincingly? – as he recalls 'the great split forward'. And he has an interesting theory on its causes.

On guard

'Contrary to what most people think and teach, Satan attacks Christians at their strong point, rather than their weak one. Most of us know where our weak points are, and we therefore tend to surround ourselves with guards at those points. For most leaders, women would be somewhere in the list of weaknesses, either high or low. Therefore the majority of us insert an ethical code in order to guard against that weak area. I personally do not counsel women by myself, and I make a point of keeping the door open when for example my secretary is with me in the office. Not because all women are unsafe in my presence, but rather as a means of strengthening my resolve to give no place to the devil.

'On the other hand, we tend to leave our strengths unguarded. After all, why spend valuable time protecting what is already strong? But we found out to our cost that what is unprotected does not remain strong for long. It is vulnerable and becomes the focus of satanic attack. The strength of the house churches was our relationships with each other. We were known for them. So while we had guards around the dangers of pride, sex and money, we were defenceless at our strong point.'

The tensions between the brothers which finally proved too strong to restrain were many and varied. Among the chief however was the handling of a case of immorality among one of the fourteen, and the so-called 'law and grace' issue. This latter debate had itself been fuelled by the publication of a booklet with the unambiguous title, *Not Under Law*. The writer was Gerald Coates, and although shunned by most Christian bookshops, some 20,000 copies were sold. The booklet was later to be incorporated in another book under the even less ambiguous title, *A Kingdom without Rules*.

To men like Arthur Wallis, it seemed to confirm the growing suspicion that Gerald and those close to him were seeking to extend the boundaries of Christian freedom beyond what was either traditional, acceptable or even biblical. The booklet and the underlying teaching behind it served also as ammunition for those outside the house-church movement who quickly and somewhat ironically labelled Gerald as a 'law to himself'. It is probably fair to say that he has not yet outgrown the reputation that he is soft on biblical standards and Christian holiness. It is an accusation he vehemently – though still chuckling – denies, contending instead that his critics have often not understood or even read his teaching; but more of that later.

Deep wounds

Gerald seems to be able to handle criticism in a relaxed sort of way: perhaps it's just as well. Or maybe it's a facade. It is clear however, that even he was stung by the letter from Arthur Wallis that led to the break-up of the 'fabulous fourteen'. Gerald felt that though the signature was Arthur's, the message was equally that of Bryn Jones.

'The accusation was that we were being motivated by a worldly and ambitious spirit, and that they could therefore no longer work with us. I have no doubt that Arthur had not the slightest idea of the ramifications of that letter when he wrote it. He would be horrified to think that twenty years later it would take centre stage in a book on the history of the house churches! It was clearly written with a view to clarifying the rapidly deteriorating situation among us. However, the effect as far as we were concerned was that churches across the country would no longer have anything to do with us. Our magazine *Fullness* was dropped like a stone. Even people we knew, who themselves had no problems with us, suddenly disappeared in the opposite direction. And of course it served to prove to our opponents, that we were no different from all the other squabbling Christians in the world.

'There were initial attempts to get us all together again

with a view to reconciliation between the brothers, but as so often happens in conflicts, the original issue soon ceased to be the present issue. It was buried under, and overtaken by, all the hard things that were said.

'The original purpose of our gathering together, first as seven, then as fourteen, had been doctrinal. Arthur had become convinced that the traditional teaching of the church concerning Christ's imminent return was flawed. That was a theological issue. But once that truth was established – at least to our satisfaction – the main concern turned from the theological to the practical. If the timing of Jesus' return was dependent on the church fulfilling God's plans on earth, how could we speed his return? This question occupied all of us. We all agreed that the restoration of the church to a position of power and glory in the earth was part of God's end-time purpose, but not everyone agreed on how these Kingdom people were to be produced, or how the prayer of Jesus in John 17 could be fulfilled. Should we call people out of the moribund denominations to join us? Or even go back and join them!'

Come together

Not surprisingly the links between Gerald and other brothers based mainly in the London area, were reinforced following the split with Arthur Wallis, Bryn Jones and those who took their side of the debate. Spurned by their erstwhile colleagues and by much of the watching church at large, the London brothers turned some-what inwards, though as Gerald recalls, to great effect. Meetings organised in the capital grew in both numb-ers and anointing until hundreds were locked out of the Albert Hall. They were crucial times of rebuilding and of rediscovering confidence. At least God had not rejected them; neither, it seemed, had many of his people.

The 1980s were years when many house-church (Gerald prefers 'new-church') leaders began to form teams of men with specific and diverse ministries to serve both local and a wider network of churches. Often referred to as 'apostolic' teams, they emerged out of the growing ministries of men such as Terry Virgo, Barney Coombs, and Tony Morton. Gerald too was active in this area, pulling together the roots that would ultimately become the Pioneer Team. Initially fairly territorial in nature, the teams have since spawned new relationships and spheres of influence in different parts of the country, not to mention in each other's territory. If the 1970s were a time of coming together, then the 1980s were largely a decade of living apart.

In touch

Deep in Gerald's spirit however, the desire for wider and renewed fellowship refused to lie low. Six years ago, and not a little nervously, he invited the leaders of apostolic teams throughout the country to come together.

'We had no agenda. Rather we just sang and prayed and waited to see what God would bring out of it. I have always felt that it is important to have both specific and general relationships. I personally need to be surrounded by those who are very close to me, for example within the Pioneer team. But I also need the not-so-close relationships of those within other new churches and non-new-church streams. Historically house churches have been good at the specific level and bad at the general. This can produce an unbalanced and isolated position. Evangelicals on the other hand, tend to be good at general relationships on a wide level, but at the expense of close, specific ones. This can lead to loneliness and a lack of real, deep fellowship.

'My motives in bringing people together, some for the first time in over ten years, was not to try to recreate what we had previously enjoyed; rather it was to seek to restore at a general level areas of relationship in an atmosphere of warmth and cordiality, and to explore ways in which we might co-operate together by combining our resources and strengths. After all we still have so much in common, as witnessed by the way in which so many of our ministries have developed along similar lines.

'Out of this have come quarterly meetings of apostolic leaders and other gatherings. They have proved useful as a forum for exchanging views and even pulpits – not that house churches have pulpits of course! Most of all they have focussed our attention on the importance and practical significance of Christian unity, which is the reaching of the nation, and indeed the nations. Though we are not now striving for the kind of uniformity of the 1970s, there is a great deal to be gained by pooling our resources and ministries in certain areas for the sake of the Kingdom of God. Perhaps that is what Jesus intended after all in John 17.'

Wet ink

Gerald Coates is not a theologian, at least not in the sense that most people define it. Like many of the new-church leaders, he has no formal Bible college training. He admits that partly as a result of this, he has not always fully thought through or developed his theology before seeking to expand it. His opponents have not been slow to highlight such shortcomings, but it would be wrong to describe Gerald as theologically naive or biblically flawed.

He is essentially in the mould of the prophet, going where no (or few!) men have dared go before. Inspiration born out of an intuitive spirit is a hallmark that has made him such a valued and sought-after speaker at Spring Harvest and other Christian events.

A prophet's life is never dull or tranquil. Though not charged simply with delivering a negative message of rebuke or chastening, he is however a challenger of existing attitudes and practices among God's people, a stick of dynamite applied to a church off track. If a prophet's task is to raise dust, Gerald has done so by the sackfull!

Chief among his insights or errors is his stance on Christian living, and particularly his emphasis on 'living from within'. It lies at the heart of the law and grace debate that fuelled the fires of division among the house-church leaders in the 1970s. What makes it so explosive is that for many Christians it challenges one of the deepest held truths in Christianity, the authority of the Bible. Take away such a pivotal aspect of the church's faith, and you might be left without a foundation. If the Bible was no longer seen as a manual for living, what is to prevent God's people from plunging headlong into an abyss of uncontrolled sin?

Still on track

As in so many other areas, Gerald has a way of disarming his critics who have at times arrived at seminars with both barrels proverbially loaded! One of his most powerful arguments is that after almost a generation of preaching the message of 'living from within', those who have sought to put the teaching into practice have not gone wholesale into error. Admittedly this is an argument from experience rather than doctrine, but it is difficult to ignore. Those who prophesied gloom and doom (and not a little judgement!) on house-church leaders for refusing to take an anti-alcohol or pro-Sabbath stance have seen rather a general relaxing of many of the traditional taboos or no-go areas of the denominations.

The question is whether this has been the thin end of the wedge or a sign of greater maturity and liberty in the church. Like many of the new-church leaders, Gerald is conscious that the long-term fruitfulness of the many radical positions adopted over the last two decades, will only be fully seen in the next generation. Yet there remains something Martin Luther-like in Gerald's determination to stand firm on living in grace.

'Jesus said that he would write his law upon our hearts. We all know that in the scriptures, "heart" means the innermost core of our being. When someone is born again, he receives a brand-new heart, a new nature, and a new spirit, which is the Holy Spirit. By fellowshipping with other believers, he or she then comes to understand how this "new life" operates, and how to sense the leading of the Holy Spirit; they then begin to live according to this new law. I use that word purposely because I want to make it clear that I am not against law itself. Jesus purposely declared that he had not come to earth to destroy the law. We would be foolish to try and do what he pointedly refused to do. But equally Jesus refused to merely rubber-stamp the path of legalism. No longer would God's words be set in stone, or even India paper! From now on it would be a law of grace and spirit written in flesh.'

Inner voice

'As far as I am concerned the Bible is not a text book,

but a test book. Nowhere in the Bible are we asked to live according to the Bible. Rather we are told to live by the Spirit. If I say that I am following Jesus whilst at the same time defrauding the tax inspector or gossiping about my brother, then you would be right to remind me that the two are incompatible. That could then be tested by the scriptures.

'Many Christians are frightened of the whole concept of living from within. They are suspicious of anything that might involve human and therefore unreliable feelings. That's why they run for the security of a Bible centred faith, and dismiss anyone who doesn't as carnal and worldly. I have often been accused of devaluing scripture, but that is the price that sometimes has to be paid by those who seek to exercise the prophetic spirit.

'In fact I have a great respect and love for the Bible. After all, don't forget that I was brought up in the Brethren! My argument is not with those who champion the cause of the authority of scripture, but with those who want to give it the degree of authority that the Bible does not seek to give itself.

'I like to compare the Bible to the bed and banks of a river. Take them away, and the water will simply dissipate. But equally, if you remove the water, you cease to have a river. The end result is the same. A river by definition is a vigorous exciting thing, not a dull, still pond that is without outlet and going nowhere.

'Many of those who have accused me of being "all river", might themselves be charged with being "all bed and bank"! How has it happened that huge chunks of the church in Britain have for years believed so passionately in the truth and power of God's word, and yet been so powerless to affect their communities for God? Perhaps, as so often happens, the pendulum has swung a little too far at times towards the river and away from the bed and banks; but only because the river had been allowed to run dry over many years, leading to dead formality instead of dynamic life.

Trust the Spirit

'The scriptures themselves lay down the principle that the sons of God are those who are led by the Spirit (Romans 8). Unfortunately the evangelical church, and even Pentecostals, have not had a very good theology about the person and work of the Holy Spirit, at least not in practice. It is one thing to believe that the Holy Spirit is a person who dwells within every believer, it is another to trust and rely on him to lead us into truth. Living from within gives the Holy Spirit the opportunity to teach and lead us in the ways of God, and to turn our lives into a vigorous, forceful river. Perhaps those who have accused me of devaluing the Bible have themselves been guilty of devaluing the person and ministry of the Holy Spirit.

'If the Holy Spirit was involved, as I believe he was, in the writing down of what we call scripture, it is only to be expected that having preserved it for some 2,000 years, he will continue to be faithful to that same body of scripture today. That's why we should be willing to test our lives against its pages. In seeking to live by the Spirit, my receiving apparatus can sometimes be faulty or impaired by the influence of sin or my flesh. At such times there is a tendency for the river to try to steer its own course; that's why there must be river banks. But they were never meant to rob the river of its intrinsic power and life.

'By and large in most areas of the world, those who live according to God's word will live a healthy and long life. The people who belong to Pioneer People and our associated churches have been taught to receive the Holy

Spirit and to live by the Spirit. If you were to take a poll of 1,000 people in Cobham and compare that group to a sample of 1,000 Pioneer People in terms of marriage break-up, child abuse, homosexuality, sexual diseases, imprisonment, criminal records, the statistics would be very different. You have to conclude that if everyone lived like those who belong to the church of Jesus, the world would be a much happier place! Such is the joy and success awaiting those who live from within.'

Law of life

Ultimately, is Gerald really saying anything that is unreasonable, or even radical? After all, if the scriptures will always confirm what the Holy Spirit will say, is it not less complicated to look into the scriptures first? Yet surely Gerald has put his finger on something of vital importance. Christianity is a relationship, not just a way of life. The whole purpose of the Christian life is to develop that relationship in a way that will bring glory to God through works of service, and fulfilment to our own lives. Our obedience to God is not an end in itself, but a means to one. Of itself it is no guarantee of a life lived near to God. Ritual without life is the stuff of sterile religion; and you wouldn't expect Gerald to have much sympathy with that.

Gerald's controversial stance on so many issues touching the church and Christian life in general has ensured a high profile for him within evangelical circles. There have been positive by-products of this; who else in Britain today could possibly have published a book of mostly witty sayings under the title of *Gerald's Quotes*? Appearances on radio and occasionally on television have become a feature of life for him. As his work for persecuted Christians with Danny Smith, and the

AIDS ministry with Patrick Dixon (ACET) have taken shape, much media attention has come Gerald's way. His somewhat glitzy way of life, rubbing shoulders with showbiz personalities like Cliff Richard, has attracted the attention of feature writers from both the Christian and secular press. He admits that he has not always handled such occasions wisely, and that the latter particularly are invariably looking for an exposé type of story. But could he really cope without the oxygen of publicity? Does he deliberately court controversy?

'I have never stood on a platform and thought, "I'm going to shock them tonight!" So I plead not guilty to controversy for its own sake. I like to be liked; that is in my nature. But it is also in the nature of the prophet to say what God wants whether or not it is what the people want to hear. The Old Testament prophets had a "burden from the Lord", which gave them little or no rest until it was delivered. Sometimes it comes with tears, at other times with a raised voice, as the prophet seeks to express the anger that God himself feels. Such things are not always appreciated, especially when they challenge the status quo either in terms of church structures or personal attitudes. Most people don't mind change as long as it leaves everything the way it is!'

On guard

'Yes, at times I have regretted some aspects of controversy. When the media telephone, they are looking for a Bakker or Swaggart story – and I'm at the top of their list! Whether it's the *Sunday Times* reporter doing a feature for their colour supplement, the James Whale show, or a programme for Brian Redhead on Radio 4, I can't help wondering whether there is a hidden agenda and whether

I am being set up. After all, I do have to protect Anona and our three sons.

'There was a phone call some time ago from the *News of the World* claiming that the paper had compromising photos of me coming out of a hotel with a woman. My response was to invite them to print them as it could have only been with my wife or Christine Noble. Of course there were no photos, and nothing materialised from the call; but it is the sort of thing that frankly I could do without.

'Over the years many things have been said or written about me which have been unflattering, unfair or in my opinion downright untrue, but you have to learn to cope with the criticism of those who either don't like you or what you are saying and doing. Some negative reaction on a personal level is inevitable when you are in the public eye, especially if you are saying things that are out of the ordinary.'

Under influence

For several years, Gerald and Anona shared their home, firstly in Cobham and later in Esher with singer Sheila Walsh and her husband Norman Miller. But it is through his long-standing friendship with Cliff Richard that Gerald has been able to influence the lives of several media personalities, though as he freely admits, with mixed results. Cliff himself is associated with Pioneer People, and has appeared in various outreach activities for the church. He is rarely, however, able to attend the services – though there is a lovely story about someone visiting Pioneer People for the first time, who went home complaining that when the congregation was asked to hold hands, he ended up next to a Cliff Richard look-alike!

Team talk

Gerald still retains a hands-on involvement in the day-to-day oversight of the Cobham-based work. However, it is his input into the lives of other leaders that is his hallmark. The national Pioneer team consists of twenty people based in different parts of the country who meet together to pray, plan, and generally strategise. Gerald's main role is to oversee this, with a particular emphasis on caring for existing churches, planting new churches, and training leaders and evangelists. TIE teams (Training in Evangelism) win hundreds to the Lord during a period of twelve months' service.

That is what Gerald calls the non-dramatic side of the work: caring for churches, training leaders, releasing ministries and planting brand-new churches using different models for inner-city, villages, and suburban areas. The eighty churches who relate to Pioneer range from small groups of fifty or sixty people to churches which are 1,000 strong. The nature of Gerald's relationship with those depends on several things. Some churches like Chichester, Southampton and Maidenhead have received a good deal of input from him.

'Some of that input may not have been public. But if you can invest your life into local church leaders, by envisioning them and helping them to resolve issues, that has a trickle-down effect into the whole church. My task is to help the churches to help themselves, not merely to fill my diary with preaching engagements.'

In the open

Nothing sums up better the present agenda and emphasis of the 'new churches' and their leaders. After almost a

generation has passed, one rarely hears the word Restoration used by men such as Gerald. The introversion
of the early years has gone, as has the tendency to arrogance typical of new movements. The narrow theological
trenches dug by early leaders have been replaced by a
more pragmatic approach. And thankfully, the isolation
of the 1970s and early 1980s – partly at least self-imposed
– has given way to a new spirit of co-operation with the
other denominations who after all might not be entirely
moribund!

Such are the signs of a maturing movement, though
not everyone within would be convinced of that. As more
denominational churches and leaders have taken on board
some of the prophetic insights the house churches have
pioneered, the old prejudices and suspicions have been
replaced by a more positive sense of co-operation which
augurs well for the future. The 'come out from among
them and join us' mentality is now very much a discarded
theory. It's a stance that Gerald feels comfortable with.

'"March for Jesus" has given Christians the opportunity
to express the love and comradeship that exists within
great sections of the evangelical church in Britain. For
one day a year, our own agendas and distinctives are put
aside as we declare that there is something that unites us
despite our differences. It is important to do this. I'm not
saying that we should ditch our distinctives, rather that we
should put them into perspective. They have often been a
source of division within the church. If you like, they have
become part of the bed and banks. March for Jesus serves
to re-emphasise the river. We must continue to strive for
the unity of John 17 in spite of our differences. Events
such as March for Jesus show that it is attainable.

'From this, we have launched Challenge 2000, a project
to nurture this groundswell of support that has been
created, into a networking of the nation with the gospel.

There is no other initiative in the UK to network the country with the gospel by the year 2000. All the other programmes are centred around individual denominations or groups, be it Baptist, Anglican or house church. Their primary interest is for their denomination, not for the body of Christ.'

Be prepared

'Jesus said in Matthew 24 that the end would come when the nations have been networked with the gospel. Who doesn't want to bring an end to this corrupt, rotten system we all live in? Someone's got to do it. This is why eschatology has always been so vital to house-church thinking. The splits and schisms that have occurred during the past twenty years have not been eschatological; they were more to do with practical issues of how to speed the Lord's return and all that will bring. If you believe that there is a fixed date in heaven for Jesus' return, then all you have to do is to keep out of as much trouble as you can. But if you believe that the church has been given a commission that must be fulfilled before Jesus' return, that determines everything you do. It is this conviction that has fuelled the energy and motivation of the new churches.

'You end up with a mission mind-set rather than a maintenance mind-set: a harvest mentality rather than a barn mentality. The man who led me to the Lord used to tell me that the Lord would come back within his lifetime; he has long since died. I cannot say when the second coming will take place, but I am clear on two things. My generation is nearer to that coming than any previous generation. And right now I am in the privileged position of being able to do what no past or future generation can do at this time. For as long as I have that opportunity I intend to make it count.'

Chapter 6

Peter Fenwick: God's gentleman

What does Peter Fenwick have in common with the eighteenth-century Methodist leader George Whitfield? Answer: they both began life in the inauspicious surroundings of a public house! In Peter's case, the hostelry in question, the Old Blue Ball, still stands some sixty-two years later. No bronze plaque outside records the event, but during his lifetime, this popular house-church leader has exercised a considerable influence on the spiritual atmosphere of his home city of Sheffield.

Although now heading up the Network team of almost thirty churches in the north of England, and exercising a wide ministry in his own right, Peter's primary burden remains the city where he grew up, graduated and has spearheaded a significant work for the Lord.

He won't enjoy reading about himself in such terms, for one of Peter Fenwick's most endearing qualities is the gentle humility that has made him so approachable by leaders of other churches and fellowships who have been seeking the wisdom and input of a father figure. But although he has been almost fully involved during the last three years in the rescue and reorganisation of one of Britain's major Christian publishers, his finger remains on the pulse of things. While his name would not figure prominently in an account of the early history of the house-church movement, Peter may well become one of the key names in setting down the agenda for the future. If so, then forty years of ministry to his native Sheffield will inevitably become something of a role model.

Peter, and indeed his wife Rita, has maintained a passion for singing from an early age. It was this interest that enticed him as a young boy to take the short walk from the public house to the local Anglican church and its choir. The church and vicar were liberal in their theology. Peter didn't know or care about this; after all, even liberal churches sing! And singing was his sole passion and joy – though as he grew older, some of the girls in the church came a close second!

New message

Peter continued to attend the church throughout his teenage years, albeit without any deep faith. When he was 19 and about to embark on a course in law and accountancy at the local university, Peter found himself confronted by a new vicar, with the rather forbidding name of Revd A. E. Geary Stevens. And a new message that centred on sin, the human heart and a personal response to Christ as Saviour. This first taste of evangelism offended him greatly, but within six months, the preaching had also affected him greatly.

'My intense dislike for the new vicar was in reality only a reaction to the deep conviction of sin that went on within me for months. I tried to reform myself and to put things right, but as I read the New Testament, I was challenged by the person of Jesus. I had never given any thought to him, and during ten years in the church I can't remember ever hearing a sermon about him. My initial feeling was that Jesus had been so arrogant; how could he claim to be the way, the resurrection, the life? I was already angry with the vicar for ruining my Sunday nights. Now I was furious with Jesus too! I vowed not to go to church again, but found that I couldn't keep away. It was tearing me apart, something had to give.

'The vicar persuaded me to go along to a youth meeting run by the now defunct National Young Life Campaign. As the evangelist Jack Ward preached the gospel, I was convicted again of my sin. But when he made an appeal for consecration – something that as an Anglican I had never seen before – I ridiculed it in my spirit as some kind of mock auction. I wanted to raise my hand and bid a fiver!

'I went home angrier than ever, but was unable to sleep that night. I flicked through John's gospel with the same questions thumping in my brain: "Is there a God?" . . . "Who is Jesus?" At about four o'clock in the morning, I began to speak out as if by revelation, "It's true . . . he is the Son of God . . . in that case I must serve him!"'

No more questions

An indescribable sense of peace filled Peter's life as he confessed Jesus as Lord. The following evening, as Jack Ward repeated his appeal, Peter Fenwick moved quickly out of his seat and went forward for counselling. In the vestry, a minister from the Calvary Holiness Church began to talk to the young enquirer. Suddenly he stopped talking and invited Peter to kneel down on the floor. As he laid his hands on Peter, the room and, more important, Peter himself, was filled with God's presence and life. He rose from his knees with the words of Ecclesiastes ringing in his ears, 'Whatever your hands find to do, do it with all your strength'. Peter knew that his search for God was over. The angry young man had become the hungry young man.

Peter took a degree in law and economics at Sheffield

University and on graduating went to work as an accountant for Tarmac Civil Engineering. Sheffield at that time
was virtually dead spiritually, with only a handful of
churches where the gospel was preached faithfully – a
far cry from its present-day counterpart in which many
flourishing churches exist side by side, with a strong
charismatic emphasis to the fore.

Together with two friends, Peter started a series of
meetings in a central location aimed at reaching young
people in the city for Christ. For twenty years, the meetings
ran on alternate Saturday evenings, with other midweek
and missionary meetings organised from time to time.
Totally interdenominational, the venture eventually had
the widespread support of the city's churches. Over the
years, some fifty young people went into missionary work
having felt the call of God in the meetings. They were
without doubt a powerful influence in the shaping of
today's evangelical church in Sheffield.

Restless spirit

Yet in the midst of this apparent success, a restlessness
gripped Peter's spirit. The young people who were being
reached were by and large from the city's middle classes,
exactly the sort of people that the churches were reaching
already. His heart ached for the young teenagers from
the council estates who seemed unreached and forgotten.
Gradually, a vision for a coffee bar ministry began to take
shape. It was ambitious, and would require a city-centre
facility. It would also be expensive.

In 1966, Peter took charge of the youth work in Sheffield
associated with the Billy Graham crusade in London, itself
beamed by black and white television relay around the
country. One day, as he passed the recently closed Athol
Hotel, Peter felt led to approach its Jewish owner.

'What do you intend doing with the hotel?' Peter enquired boldly.

'That's none of your business,' came the curt reply.

'No, but it might be God's business,' Peter retorted.

'You're not a Jew. Why should I be talking to you?'

'Well, I want to borrow it for some youth meetings.'

'How much are you going to pay?' asked the business-man casually.

'Oh nothing,' countered Peter, 'but if you leave it empty it will soon be vandalised.'

Unable to argue with this logic, the owner agreed to let the premises for a few weeks, which eventually became three months. As 1,500 young people packed into the hotel every night, it was obvious that a longer-term facility such as a coffee bar was now sorely needed. The name 'Mustard Seed' was adopted by those who shared the vision with Peter, but it would need a miracle of God's provision to bring it into being. As a weary Peter and Rita Fenwick gratefully accepted the offer of a holiday following the period at the Athol Hotel, they little realised that the answer was already taking shape.

Mysterious ways

Jock Stein had worked alongside Peter in an outreach to young people on the housing estate where Peter had been born. A generous, unpretentious man, he was employed in the steel industry and had become a good friend. He kindly offered to drive the couple up to his mother's holiday cottage in the Cairngorms. It seemed unlikely that the man with an old Morris Traveller would become a key player in the coffee bar scenario. But as Peter dozed in the car, Jock took up the conversation.

'Have you ever heard of Stein's Refractory Bricks?' he asked quietly.

'Of course,' Peter replied. 'Are you part of that?'

'Well yes,' he continued slightly embarrassed. 'It was my grandfather's firm, then my father's, and now you could say that it virtually belongs to me.'

By now Peter was wide awake, recalling how he and Jock had prayed together for the £40,000 that would be needed in order to finance the coffee bar.

'Obviously, I could finance the whole venture,' he continued, 'but I need to know whether that is what God wants. So I have put out a fleece, by putting up for sale some shares that I own in Rubery Owen. If they realise £40,000 after commissions and expenses, I will know that it is for the coffee bar.'

Peter's face dropped slightly, as he contemplated the ups and downs of the stock exchange. He couldn't disagree with Jock's theology, but felt like a hostage to fortune. Within a short time however, the required amount of money was forthcoming and the 'mustard seed' was planted in the shadow of the town hall. The premises were ideal for a daytime restaurant which could become a coffee bar at night. Now that his prayers had been answered, Peter would be able to go back to being a well-paid accountant and family man.

Ready and willing

The trustees began to look for a suitable person to manage and oversee the project. In their hearts they knew who they wanted, and needed. But no one had the courage to approach the man who had received the burden from the Lord in the first place. A succession of names was mooted for the post, but each proved unsuitable for a variety of reasons. Finally, and with a certain amount of trepidation, the chairman turned to Peter and asked whether he was willing to take on the full-time responsibility. He needn't have worried: Peter's answer was immediate and positive, especially since he had already talked through with Rita the prospect of him becoming a poorly paid minister of the gospel!

The Mustard Seed opened every day except Sunday for five years as a centre of evangelism, counselling and pastoral care. During that time the number of direct converts was not immense, though some were particularly significant. Like Paul Stephens, who already had a serious criminal record when Peter and the team at the Mustard Seed came into contact with him. After several years of sharing Jesus with him, interspersed by periods in prison, Paul was remarkably converted. Today he serves as an elder alongside Peter in the Central House Church in Sheffield.

A team of 100 volunteers worked alongside Peter in the interdenominational venture. The policy concerning converts was simple: they were taken by the contact person to his or her own church and introduced to that church. In this way, converts did not have to make contact with a local church by themselves: that might follow later.

Over and out

In fact, Peter was already experiencing the effect that the church can have on those who come to Christ in a non-church setting. On many occasions he took the predominantly working-class young people into the evangelical Anglican church where he and Rita worshipped. Almost without exception, they never returned. Overcome by the awesomeness of the building, and ill at ease with the traditions and the formality of the services, it all seemed a million miles from the laid back, non-religious atmosphere of the coffee bar. The trustees decided to invite all the city's clergy together in order to share the problem with them. It was to prove prophetic, both in terms of the coffee bar ministry, and more important, in Peter's own life.

First, however, he had to sit through the scathing criticism of some of the city's evangelical leaders, one of whom was appalled by the use of drama and some middle of the road pop and folk music in the coffee bar.

'This is not the house of God,' he thundered, 'this is the gateway to hell!'

Peter was still recoiling from the shock of this when another evangelical entered the fray.

'It is very obvious that these are only superficial conversions if they won't join themselves to any of our churches.'

As a sense of gloom and negativism descended over the meeting, and especially over Peter, an unlikely source of help rose to his feet. Canon Gerald Hollis had arrived at the meeting as the representative of the bishop. He had already taken an interest in the coffee bar work, and had invited Peter to speak about it in various settings including the chamber of commerce. Gerald took the evangelical leaders to task for their biting criticism.

'I am deeply thankful,' he interjected, 'that I am not an evangelical. You are so good at shooting each other. I have something to say to the committee, and to you, Peter, in particular. Your problem is that you don't work in a biblical fashion.'

A sense of incredulity – and of slight annoyance – became almost tangible as the city's evangelical leaders found themselves being lectured on biblical Christianity by a somewhat liberal Anglican canon.

'I'm very serious,' he continued; 'you place no value on the church. You are zealous in getting people converted and hooking them up to God, but the church has a low priority. Because your work in the coffee bar is divorced from the church, the latter has no relevance for those you come into contact with. Until you meet as a church in this building, you will never succeed.'

Staying together

To say the least, the suggestion went down like a lead balloon! Even to Peter himself, it was unthinkable. All that he had been involved with in the city over many years had been on an interdenominational basis. He saw his work as a bridge builder, preparing new Christians for contact with existing churches. He had never considered starting a church himself. This was certainly part of the reason why he had been able to maintain the support of other leaders and churches. He dismissed the prospect out of hand. Eventually a compromise was reached which Peter felt he could live with. He would hold a service on Sunday evenings in the coffee bar, providing that it was adopted by his Anglican church as an official part of its outreach. He was determined to resist at all costs the option to go it alone.

Rita wasn't quite so sure. Peter's full-time involvement in ministry often left her and their children by themselves in the Anglican church. She felt that this was having an adverse effect on their children's spiritual welfare. The vicar wasn't too sure either. He soon began to come under pressure within the church concerning the coffee bar meeting. When was Peter Fenwick going to bring his young people into the church? As numbers grew quickly to about fifty people, Peter started to come to the conclusion, slowly and reluctantly, that the answer was probably never. The informal meetings in the welcoming familiar surroundings of the coffee bar were a different world from that of a traditional church service. There was no going back. When Peter's vicar informed him of the church's intention to cut the new work loose, it was the final confirmation that Peter needed. It was time to set sail.

Missing link

The coffee bar ministry lasted for five years after which the premises were compulsorily purchased by the local council. But by that time, the mustard seed had become a church plant, with a charismatic flower. The story of how Peter himself was baptised in the Spirit as a prelude to leading his fledgling church into the same experience, is best told in his own words. It contains many of the elements that will be familiar to other Christians who have found themselves treading a similar path during two decades of charismatic renewal: rejection of charismatic phenomena, confusion, curiosity and desperation. As so often happens, God used another Christian to point Peter in the right direction. Dave France had worked alongside Peter during the outreach in the Athol Hotel. When Peter heard reports of strange happenings in the Plymouth Brethren in Rotherham, associated with the name of Dave France, he decided to go and have a look. It proved a right decision.

'Dave had begun to exercise the gifts of the Spirit among the young people in the Plymouth Brethren. Eventually they were excluded from the Brethren assembly because of their behaviour. I was confused by it all, but one thing kept nagging away at me: Dave France was a man of God, who would not be duped.

'My secretary at work bought me the book, *Nine O'Clock in the Morning*. This only served to increase my confusion. As I analysed my own experience since my conversion, it seemed to me that I had experienced everything that the author included in the baptism of the Spirit, except speaking in tongues. I had prayed for the sick, and during the coffee bar ministry had often felt that I was using words of knowledge in specific situations. Perhaps I had been baptised in the Spirit when the Holiness minister laid his hands on me the night I was converted. It had certainly been a memorable experience of meeting with God. But why no tongues?

'I had already met people like John Noble, Gerald Coates, and Maurice Smith. John kindly invited me to a conference held at the WEC centre. About forty leaders from emerging house churches were present. On the Sunday morning, as we broke bread and worshipped, I found myself singing in tongues. I had been a Christian for twenty-five years, and unknown to me I had been baptised in the Spirit during my very first encounter with God. But it had taken all those years for me to enter into the fullness of that experience.'

Time to choose

The closing of the coffee bar as a result of compulsory purchase inevitably thrust the fellowship into a time of decision-making. It soon became clear that alternative premises would not become available: the future lay elsewhere. And for Peter, the time had come to turn his back once and for all on the security of an accountant's salary. When the church offered to support him financially, Peter hesitated. After all, most were young people, and only a small number had paid jobs. Finally he agreed to their request to give them a chance. They didn't let him and Rita down.

Like so many local leaders at that time, Peter had no formal Bible training, limited experience of running a church, and he felt fairly isolated. A number of local men had taken an interest in his work over the years, including Rotherham pastor David Powell, who at key times had given words of knowledge concerning the coffee bar and who had arranged for Peter to meet David Wilkerson during a visit to Britain, and Independent Calvinist Doug Higgins who has become a lifelong friend and influence. Forty years before, when Peter took on the leadership of the youth work, Doug had been challenged by a word from the then leader Keith Hood:

'I want you to be a father to this man.' Doug was in tears as he took on what he felt was God's task for him. For twenty years he poured his life into Peter.

'I'm just the oil rag,' he said to Peter, 'whenever you need it, I'll be there.' Doug is eighty years of age now and as vigorous for God as ever.

Long distance

Peter continued to enjoy fellowship with Gerald Coates and John Noble, but at a distance. What he really needed was someone who he could relate to on a leadership level within the house churches, but who didn't live in London! When a colleague suggested Peter Parris, who worked with Bryn Jones in Bradford, it seemed an ideal relationship. But when the division between the house-church leaders took place in the late 1970s, Peter Fenwick found himself in the middle of what he describes as a 'web of intrigue and untruths'.

He soon came under considerable pressure to break off all contacts with the London group of brothers, for no other reason than that Peter Parris was staying with Bryn Jones; therefore Peter Fenwick should do the same. In effect he was being asked to place loyalty higher than truth.

It was an unsavoury episode which perhaps typifies what was happening at the time. Men whose ministries were both gifted and anointed found themselves adopting practices and attitudes every bit as bad as those they had highlighted in the denominations. As half-truths and untruths circulated, Peter went to visit Arthur Wallis himself in order to ascertain the truth. It became clear to him that what he had heard concerning the London brothers was not a true account. Peter Fenwick's brief flirtation with the 'R1' group of men was at an end. It would only be right, however, to say that many relationships have since been restored, albeit at a different level.

Church share

For the last fifteen years, Sheffield House Church has used the United Reformed Church building opposite the Crucible Theatre for its Sunday afternoon meeting. It has been an excellent arrangement for both parties. After outgrowing eleven venues during the first two years after the Mustard Seed closed, it provided at least a temporary opportunity to draw breath. But when the numbers reached 350, the absolute limit of the URC building, it was time for the next phase of the church's development – planting out new fellowships in other areas of Sheffield.

Altogether five groups have been established from the central church in areas of Sheffield where there were no existing evangelical churches. In addition, two other groups have severed themselves from the main body in what Peter tactfully describes as 'self-sets'.

As you might expect, Peter has handled the new church plants with both a hands-on and hands-off approach. The policy he has adopted is to give a new group its own finances and to appoint elders to take on the responsibility for the work at the earliest possible time, often about a year after its inception. Like many of the house-church leaders who have moved along similar lines, he has had to tread a fine line, so as to neither abandon or smother the fledgling works. He confesses that the policy has caused him more than a little pain at times.

'Since we appointed elders to oversee the welfare of the church plants, I have remained available for fellowship and counsel along with Geoff Williams, a fellow elder and missionary statesman. The churches utilise that facility as they wish. I would still feel, however, that I have a right to intervene among them if I felt it was necessary. The elders could of course throw me out: that seems to have been how the Apostle Paul operated in the churches he founded. He didn't govern them, but he retained the right to tell them to get their act together or else!'

With hindsight

'Two of the five new churches have developed in a fairly independent way; both are doing well. Obviously I receive a lot of joy and satisfaction from seeing churches and their leaders grow up into a place of maturity and strength. But my feelings are tinged with regret that we have not all stayed closer together. There would have been about 800 of us now, and in a large city that sort of size can be very helpful. Having said that, it is possible that we might not have reached that number if we had not adopted an open policy. But it's a policy that has caused me some pain from time to time. I sometimes wish that I hadn't let go as quickly as I did. But I also know that it was the right thing for me to do personally. Since the root cause of that pain was my desire to implement New Testament practices, I cannot dwell on my regrets.'

There are unlikely to be any further church plants from Central House Church in the foreseeable future. During the last fifteen months, the church has plateaued somewhat. Indeed the largest of the related churches is now the 300-strong King Centre in Nether Edge. It's not difficult to see a link between that and Peter's almost full-time involvement during that period with the restructuring of Kingsway Publications. He was persuaded six years ago by Gilbert Kirby to become a trustee of that organisation, on the understanding that it would involve only a small commitment of time! Peter had been out of business management for twenty-five years, but it soon became obvious to him that all was not well with the company. The commitment and skills of the workforce could not be faulted, but his accountant's eye quickly found that a financial catastrophe was waiting in the wings. When a fire swept through the STL warehouse, destroying all the stock of Kingsway, it seemed that all might be lost. Yet as so often happens, the ashes became the starting point for a complete re-evaluation and revamping of the company.

Peter initially agreed to undertake a three-month analysis of the company's state of affairs, and in particular its financial viability. It was to last for fifteen months which were both exacting and exciting.

On the brink

On many occasions staff were called together to pray through periods of crisis and decision making. Eventually, in what seems to have been God's intervention, an arrangement was reached with an American religious publisher which should ensure the long-term viability of Kingsway, provide a market for its products in the USA, and avoid the fate of other Christian companies in Britain, which have been swallowed up within large American secular organisations.

It was an experience that Peter would not have missed

for the world. But he did miss the close involvement with the Sheffield church during that time. And they missed him. It remains to be seen whether Peter will once again feel that it is right for him to throw most of his energy back into local church leadership, or whether like some of the other brothers, he will develop his wider ministry as a father figure to almost thirty churches who are part of the Network group of fellowships.

Most of the related churches are in the north of England. In keeping with this most laid-back of house-church leaders the links between themselves and Peter are simply ones of friendship, devoid of financial or governmental constraints.

'I do not have a superintendent type role within Network. Neither do I have to visit all the churches regularly to make sure they remain loyal. Those who are involved with us are entirely free to plough their own furrow in God. If I may say so humbly, this is one of the things that distinguishes us from most denominations. I am not anti-denominational. My background was in inter-denominational ministry and we have excellent relationships with other churches in Sheffield. A couple who came to us from an Anglican church actually came with the blessing of the bishop! Similarly we have transferred people with our blessing to denominational churches. But I would resist personally the trappings that tend to go with belonging to a denomination. Some of our churches would like a more up-front organisation, publishing its own literature etc., but I would not want to lose the essential ingredient of a relationship based on a spiritual sense of belonging.

'We must avoid becoming blinkered. There is an enormous amount of cross-pollination that takes place among us, as churches receive input and ministry from each other. But we discourage all our fellowships from thinking that all their needs can be met within Network. The whole counsel of God has not been vouchsafed to any one group. The older I get, the more wisdom I see in that.

'The Network leaders come together three times a year to pray, plan and share as brothers. From time to time we ask the churches to consider contributing to specific projects that might require the resources of several rather than one fellowship. But it is a free-will matter, with no brownie points for the generous, or black marks for those who may not wish to respond.

'There is a core team of men whose ministries and gifts are available to the churches. We tried initially to avoid using the word "team" in case it sounded hierarchical or elitist. Similarly we have always been wary of terms such as "covering" to describe the kind of relationship that exists between the team and the churches. "Roles of responsible care" is a term that I am much happier with. The expectation is, that a related church will grow up partly as a result of that care, and will therefore need us less as time goes by.'

Good advice

A good example of how this works in practice is to be found in the north-east of England. Brian Howells was a Presbyterian layman in charge of a detached group of Presbyterian believers when he first met Peter. Non-charismatic and very isolated, he was advised by several people in the church who had met Peter, to get in touch. Finally, and with some trepidation, he invited Peter to spend a weekend with him and the church. On the Sunday evening, a serious pastoral problem erupted that devastated Brian. As a visiting speaker, Peter was able to take a more detached view of this situation.

'This is what you must do,' he counselled, in a tone that was both authoritative and yet non-threatening. 'And you must do it tonight. We'll go back to your home and have some prayer for you.'

When Brian came through the front door at 1 a.m., the last thing he expected was to see Peter and his colleague still waiting for him. In fact it was another two hours before they set out on the return journey to Sheffield. It had surely been in the purposes of God that Peter had been invited during that weekend. In the midst of a crisis, a relationship of trust and respect was born.

Within days, Brian telephoned Peter wanting to come down and talk with him about the baptism in the Spirit. It was arranged that he come and spend a weekend in Sheffield. He had not however counted on going to the Sunday afternoon service with his hosts. As he sat in the meeting, exposed to a form of worship and a liberty of expression that he had never experienced before, his fears evaporated. Sitting quietly in the meeting, he ceased to be a spectator and became a participant as the Holy Spirit fell on him.

From that point things developed quickly. Groups of people from Sheffield, including musicians, travelled to the North-east to get alongside the local believers. And a number of people made the journey south to be exposed to life within the Sheffield congregation. For about three years, Peter visited the church at least five times a year, not merely to preach, but to share his wisdom and experience with the church and its leader. As both grew stronger, Peter's input reduced. For three years there was no active involvement between Peter and the Gateshead church. During that time Brian developed more local links with, among others, Pentecostal pastor Herbert Harrison. But when a leadership problem blew up just months ago, it was to Peter that Brian turned once more. After all, that is what friends are for.

Into the future

And Peter Fenwick has many friends, particularly in Sheffield where, after forty years, he retains a passion for the church; not just for his church, but for God's. He is not merely a man looking back nostalgically, reminiscing over past experiences and successes; he has clearly defined goals for the future, whether or not they will be achieved in his lifetime. In a city with two of the leading evangelical Anglican churches in Britain, Peter wants to see an ever-increasing sense of co-operation among church leaders, regardless of denominational label.

'There are lots of good things happening in many of the denominations. That is to be welcomed, and local churches will quite rightly want to line up with the national initiative and goals of their grouping. But we shouldn't allow this to blind us to God's strategy for the cities of our land. They cannot be won to Christ by one church or by one leader; still less by one denomination. We need each other for that, and in particular a united church working together for the sake of the gospel.

'When Billy Graham held a mission in Sheffield some years ago, we reached a point of co-operation and relationship whereby churches and their leaders positively rejoiced in each other's success. There was no competition, no mad scramble for converts. It drained away eventually, but lasted long enough to convince me that it is possible. If we can engender this kind of spirit on special occasions, why can we not do the same on a continued basis? I have no doubt, that if and when that happens, Sheffield will really sit up and take notice. I don't believe that Jesus' prayer for unity will fall to the ground. If that were to happen, what hope would there be for my prayers?

'The kind of co-operation I am talking about, will only come to pass when leaders consider other men better than themselves in terms of godliness. Styles of worship and oversight structures are not the hurdles that we must overcome. Unity is an issue of the heart, not of the theology book. That doesn't make truth unimportant; it simply makes me more aware that I might not have a monopoly of God's counsel.

'After forty years, I'm convinced that eldership is the correct governmental structure for us. But I can't write off the Baptists, Presbyterians, or Anglicans because they operate differently. Neither can I be satisfied with a bogus unity. A couple who moved from our fellowship to work in ministry within an Anglican church in the city, had to submit themselves to re-baptism and confirmation, despite being bone fide, tried and tested, Spirit-filled believers. When that ceases to happen, then I will know that we are really getting to where we need to be.'

At a time of life when most people, Christians included, are looking to take life easier with an eye on retirement, Peter shows no sign of allowing his vision to become sidetracked by the cosy prospect of a pension book and free bus pass – despite his being a non-driver!

One suspects that the vast experience of a lifetime's ministry will continue to find a ready outlet in the lives of churches and especially their leaders. His soft voice grows noticeably more forceful as he contemplates what lies ahead.

'There remains a lot to be done. We must set ourselves to achieve Christ's goals for his church. Since my conversion, I have always expected great things from God. The past two decades have shown us that Jesus is still very interested in his church. So much of the New Testament is optimistic about the church. I have never taken on board the view that the church would survive in the last days – but only just.

'That is to give Satan too much authority and influence. God will have the last word, not his arch-enemy. I believe that the best days for the church lie in front of us, not behind us. The future will be greater than the past. The priority now for all of us is to ensure that we become part of that glorious future. It is not enough to have been part of the past.'

Chapter 7

John Noble: Bridge-builder extraordinaire

'The Lord wants you to establish a father figure within the Pioneer team.'

The speaker was American preacher Dale Gentry, the occasion a visit to Gerald Coates' Cobham fellowship in 1990. Gerald was used to people trying to tell him what to do, but this word was different: it had a impact that was both immediate and long lasting. It didn't take him long however to settle in his heart who that father figure should be. For many years he had valued his close friend John Noble in such a way. But how would the bearded leader of the Essex based Team Spirit group of churches respond to the suggestion of leaving his present sphere of ministry in order to join Pioneer?

Gerald needn't have worried. The Lord had already begun a work of preparation in the hearts of John and his wife Christine. It was time to put their eight-bedroomed, much extended terraced house in Collier Row up for sale.

John's heavy east London accent may betray his family origins, but in fact his early life was spent very much in transit as he moved around with his Salvation Army officer father. He attended seven different schools before the age of 11 when the family ended up in Essex. Although his father died when John was only 16, the roots of Christianity and in particular of the Salvation Army had already been laid in him. But John was to walk a tortuous route before finally committing himself to the service of Christ.

'My grandparents on my father's side and my maternal grandmother were all deeply committed to the Salvation Army. They had been involved during the lifetime of William Booth, so I grew up listening to their stories of Army life at its best. After my father died, things started to deteriorate in my life. By the time I entered the Irish Guards to do my two years of National Service, I was drinking, smoking and beginning to dabble in occult-type activity. My sister had introduced me to ouija board parties, and while in the guards we would play with the board in the barrack room. So much so that I was nicknamed "the ghost man".

'Spiritual experiences and supernatural happenings became part and parcel of my everyday life. Eventually, my search for spiritual truth and reality would lead me back to Christ, but at that time predicting the future, looking into the past, and generally dabbling in all things occult became my overriding passion.'

Two's company

About that time, John met Christine. They soon discovered that they had much in common, not least an interest in the paranormal. Christine's mother, though nominally Anglican, was in fact deeply superstitious and occultic. Fortune telling and seances dominated the family. In her search for the supernatural, she used to trudge around the various churches with Christine in tow. When she failed to find what she was looking for in the church, she would wend her way back to the sources of occult activity. It was hardly a promising start for someone who was to become not only the wife of John, but a recognised minister in her own right and frequent speaker at Spring Harvest.

No prizes for guessing what happened next. The couple began to practise spiritism together. While other couples were dating at the cinema or dance hall, John and Christine were attending a seance with its manifestations of writing and flying objects. They started using the ouija board together. Then one day, the devil took a step too far. During an ouija session, the glass challenged the couple to say the Lord's Prayer backwards. Not only could John not bring himself to do that, but he became convinced of the power with which he was co-operating. If the devil was so real, then perhaps it was time to start seeking God again!

As John and Christine started reading the Bible together, they were struck by the way in which Jesus delivered people from evil spirits. It was to be a turning point in their lives. Never again would they doubt the reality of spiritual forces. Nor would they be satisfied with any experience that did not have Jesus as its focal point. They were hungry for reality. They found it in the supermarket.

'We met a Bible-believing Baptist couple in the supermarket at the end of our road. He was a man of simple faith, and though not baptised in the Spirit, he believed in the miracles that Jesus and the apostles did. He befriended us and proceeded to disciple us in the ways of the Lord. Then we heard about an outpouring of the Spirit in a little mission in Three Colts Lane in Bethnal Green. The brother who was leading the work and who had opposed the baptism in the Spirit for many years, had himself been filled with the Spirit and was now praying for others. Hundreds of people from all kinds of denominations came to be prayed for. I went along with this Baptist brother and was filled with the Spirit. I was so excited; for two hours I laughed, cried, and spoke in tongues. Just round the corner from where Booth had started

his Salvation Army, I knew that I too had found my
destiny.'

Free at last

Not that Satan had yet finished with John and Christine.
One evening as they sat peacefully at home, Christine
felt a tightening in her throat and chest. It was as if a
pair of hands was seeking to squeeze all life from her.
It quickly became obvious that the source of the problem
was supernatural, not physical. Without knowing quite
what was going on, or how to resolve it, the couple
stood together and began to praise God in tongues. As
they did so, the sinister presence and its manifestations
began to withdraw and leave the room. The battle was
over, the power of evil that had built up during the days
of occult activity had been broken. As John and Christine
went through the whole house praying over their children
and in every room, they thanked God for his grace. There
would be many other battles, but the war had been won.

Convinced that God wanted him to use his new-found
freedom in a miraculous way, John began with a somewhat
naive enthusiasm to look for possible areas of ministry.
Raising the dead seemed a good starting point, but in the
absence of any likely candidates to hand, he sought out an
elderly lady who was nearly dead and he prayed in faith
over her. The results were not encouraging, particularly
for the lady. She died within three days, but since she was
a Christian, she was at least, so to speak, insured!

Not to be put off however by this inauspicious start,
John found two other elderly ladies also in poor health.
He anointed them with oil, solemnly laid his hands on
them according to the scriptures, and commanded them
to be made whole. Sadly they too were promoted to glory!
By now thoroughly deflated – and, one suspects, carefully

avoided by elderly ladies – John began to ask the Lord some pertinent questions. Why was he so impotent in terms of miraculous power, when he had received the power of the Holy Spirit into his life? To a man who had experienced supernatural phenomena in his unsaved state, it was doubly disconcerting.

'The Lord showed me in various ways that first and foremost I had been called to a life of obedience, and that not only was obedience more important than miracle power, it was also the route to it. Hence the emphasis in the New Testament on Jesus' obedience to the Father during his ministry on earth. I had read both about the character and charisma of Jesus in the scriptures, but I had not fully understood the vital link between the two. In the same way that Jesus had overcome sin and Satan in the desert before beginning to move in the power of the Holy Spirit, so I was being called to live a holy life and to expect God's power to accompany that. I had assumed, as so many Christians do, that my receiving the Holy Spirit in some way gave me an automatic authority over Satan and his works. In fact as with Jesus himself, the battle against sin, flesh and the devil can only be won by those who are already filled. Up to that point, God had got hold of me; but I needed to get hold of him.

'I rapidly read the Bible over and over again. From every page the church seemed to jump out at me. But it was a church unlike anything I had known. Instead of being bogged down by constitutions and buildings and unnecessary ritual, it was fluid, mobile, and dynamic.'

Role model

It would be at least six years before the seeds of what he was discovering in scripture finally germinated into a burden from the Lord to create a working model in Essex based on New Testament principles. But first, however, some more pieces of God's jigsaw for his life had to be put together. John began to share his testimony and move around in ministry among churches of all denominations in the Ilford area. Not surprisingly his testimony was well received in coffee bars, schools and colleges. He taught in Bible class in a non-denominational Sunday school and attended the tin hut Salvation Army meeting on a regular basis. But increasingly as he visited various churches, John began to develop relationships with a wide range of Christians including Norman Barnes at the local Pentecostal church. This was to lead to the formation of an evangelistic team for street and beach work. But after several years of itinerating in this way, a sense of frustration started to set in.

'I had been preaching about the baptism in the Holy Spirit and my understanding of the church for about six years in various denominational fellowships. I had said some very radical things during that time, but to my consternation no one seemed to mind. I would perhaps suggest the possibility of getting rid of pews or worshipping in a totally different way. Everyone would say a hearty "Amen", and ask me back in three months' time. But nobody wanted to do or change anything. All they wanted was to fill their pulpit on a Sunday.

'During that time I read Watchman Nee's *The Normal Christian Church Life*, which I believe was never published in this country. It confirmed everything I believed and had been teaching about the church. I bemoaned my situation to the Lord. What was I to do when confronted with such radical truth and such immovable hearers? The answer was not long in coming.'

John and Christine felt led to open their home as a place

of fellowship. Several people from the Bible class where John taught came along and were baptised in the Spirit. Also a group of young people began to meet together. It seemed as if a constant stream of needy, seeking people was wending its way to the home. Many were counselled by Christine as she took her place alongside John in his ministry. It's a partnership that has continued ever since, even to the extent of writing alternate chapters in a book on the Holy Spirit. Their commitment to using their home as a base for spiritual surgery has also endured the passage of time. For much of their married life they have lived in an extended family situation along with their five children.

Locked out

But as the Noble front door began to open to a wider group of people, many other doors started to close. Banged shut might be a better description. In what was a hurtful time, John found himself the victim of that curious Christian tendency to view as suspicious or even dangerous, anything that is out of the ordinary. Rumours about what was going on in John's home and ministry – not to mention on his chin – abounded. Even some of his closest Christian friends became 'unavailable'.

'It was as if we had committed some heinous public sin. Every opportunity for public ministry ceased overnight as the rumour-mongering gathered speed. The kindest were that we had gone off the rails, while others accused me of preaching a doctrine of British Israelism. Loaded questions such as 'What do they do behind closed doors?' or 'Is it true that men dance with other men?' were certain to deepen the level of suspicion, and further the degree of isolation that we were feeling. As usually happens in such cases, the people who were stating and spreading the rumours made no attempt to have any meaningful contact with us. When the news got round that I had grown a beard, it merely served to confirm how off-track I really was. It goes without saying of course, that Jesus was clean shaven!

'The only person who publicly defended us was Brian Richardson from the Elim movement. He wisely took the Gamaliel approach, that if what we were doing was of God, it would prosper. Brian has remained a friend of ours since and certainly we were encouraged by his refusal to jump on the bandwagon of criticism that was hitting us from every direction.

'I have always had a heart for the denominations, never more so than today. During the early 1960s we had a series of meetings in the Elim church in Ilford which for those days were quite historic. Called "The work of the Holy Spirit in the Church Today", the non-denominational meetings filled the 400-seat hall every Tuesday for six weeks under the ministry of Michael Harper, George Forester, Campbell MacAlpine and others. It was clear that we were touching something very close to God's heart, but when we started meeting in our home, all this stopped. By this time however, the seeds of a vision from the Lord had been sown in me, and I suspect in many others. For over thirty years since then, I have never doubted that there would emerge in the last days, a united remnant church made up from every stream and nation, that would represent Jesus as an image of him on earth. Only in this way will he be seen by the world in his true character and power.'

In the Spirit

The fellowship meeting in John and Christine's home originally numbered just a handful. It quickly grew to about thirty-five people, at which point numbers levelled off. The church was presumably coming up against what writers on church growth call the goldfish bowl syndrome, whereby churches tend to stop growing numerically when their buildings or places of worship become three-quarters full. John's house church was certainly way beyond that figure when the decision was made to look for a public building in which to meet. Perhaps predictably, and possibly even a touch mischievously, this unorthodox group began meeting in a public house. The worst suspicions of John's critics seemed to have been confirmed as the upstairs room in the 'Cauliflower and Seven Kings' echoed to the sound of loud music, raucous singing and footstamping dance, as well as the more gentle art of drama and dance movement, organised by RADA-trained Christine.

'The meetings were bursting with creativity. Almost everyone would sing in the Spirit and many prophesy and minister in various ways. It was spontaneous, dynamic and very exciting. In many respects, our rejection by the other churches actually became a blessing in disguise, spurring us on to something fresh in God. We were free to develop our own ethos without people breathing down our necks. It was as if the Lord had cut us off so that we could find our identity.

'During our time in the pub, we grew to about 120 people. Many others would visit from other churches. Some were like the Baptist brother who had a list of criticisms he wanted answering. After three weeks he told me that he had crossed all of them off his list, and he gave us a clean bill of health. Most of those who came to look didn't come back. We were quite relaxed about this, having determined never to invite or ask anyone from another fellowship to join us.'

The early 1970s were key years for the house churches in terms of building relationships. Most groups, John's included, had paddled their own canoe often through uncertain, even turbulent waters. Unaware of the fact that the Holy Spirit was raising up similar groups in the evangelical undergrowth, many were genuinely amazed to discover that in many towns and cities, new fellowships with similar aspirations were finding their feet. John met Peter Lyne at one of Denis Clarke's Prayer and Bible Weeks. Maurice Smith and a youthful Gerald Coates also became his firm friends. From thinking that his was the only group in the whole land with such a radical agenda, John now discovered many of like mind and heart. Key teachings of the day centred on the church as a means by which God's Kingdom would become visible on earth; law and grace; creativity in worship; and relationships with other brothers.

Cut off from the sources of fellowship that had once meant so much to him, John eagerly devoured the teaching and input of men whose names read like a charismatic who's who: Campbell MacAlpine, Arthur Wallis, Denis Clarke, Michael Harper and Cecil Cousen.

'Cecil was very close to us and for a period of time came to stay in our home. He prophesied over a small group of us when we were absolute nobodies, that from us there would come apostles and prophets. He also preached a lot on grace and laid a vital foundation in my life and others. Within our own orbit, Maurice Smith was a great influence on me; not because he taught me new things, but he made me face up to what I believed, and to voice it. This was particularly so on the law and grace issue. We were hammered by our critics for supposedly encouraging people to behave in a non-Christian, non-biblical manner. I don't believe that we ever did that. Rather we were open and up-front about issues that nobody else wanted to talk about – though they often did them!

'I was the seventh brother to be invited by Arthur Wallis to discuss eschatology at his home. Originally there were six, and Bryn Jones prophesied that they were to meet three times and that the number should be seven. As our relationships developed, we committed ourselves to an openness and reality with each other. Most of the time we talked about theology, but I wanted to know equally about people's experiences in areas like sexuality. Our young people need to know what their leaders think on such issues. For that reason, I have taken every opportunity since to speak on family life and sexuality. There must be no hidden agenda in church and Christian life. They become opportunities for Satan, as was sadly the case when division ultimately came among us.'

Poles apart

It has been hinted elsewhere, notably in Andrew Walker's *Restoring the Kingdom*, that a personality clash between John and Bryn Jones was one of the major issues that divided the Restorationists in the 1970s. After nearly twenty years, neither is keen to rake over the ashes on a personal level. One suspects however that there was something of the irresistible object and the immovable force in their relationship. While the years may have mellowed both, they remain today men of strong opinion. Even Christine described John as 'strongly opinionated' in a book they produced together!

Like all of the brothers, John has considered views and perspectives on what Gerald Coates called, 'the great split forward'. They deserve to be recorded, not only as a perspective on history, but as a positive contribution to all those interested in the area of relationships.

'I felt a great deal of frustration at the time, because there is no doubt that together we were a power to be reckoned with. When we divided, a lot of people who had been challenged by various issues got off the hook. I don't believe what happened was right, but I am equally certain that God uses whatever we bring to him, even our weaknesses and failures.

'The division undoubtedly broke our strength as a group together, but a positive result of this was that in a strange way the blessing and revelation that we had received became available to a wider body of God's people. If we had remained together, there might have been a strength that would have polarised and alienated a lot of other people. We are not now by and large perceived as a threat by the evangelical and charismatic communities, and this in turn has led to a good degree of co-operation among us that might not have been possible, and which we ourselves would probably not have looked for if we had remained intact. It was very much a case of our strength being made perfect through weakness. I feel very comfortable with where we are now.

'I have no doubt that Arthur Wallis did what he did out of conscience, and for the very best reasons. I wouldn't have said that about everyone at the time. I must confess also that as I have gone on with the Lord, I have become conscious of my own character weaknesses. My determination to be honest and open sometimes meant that I was like a dog with a bone who wouldn't let go; perhaps it would have been wiser and more gracious to have stated my point of view and then left it on the table. Looking back I can see how this particularly antagonised Bryn and I regret doing this. I also regret that as relationships with other men have been restored, Bryn has not felt able to become a major player in this. I hope that will alter in the course of time.'

No extremes

'There was admittedly some genuine concern at the time,

as to where the teachings that I and others espoused on grace would lead. Don't forget that it was in many respects uncharted territory. Men of integrity like Arthur were fearful lest we were being led by demonic spirits into the kind of freedom that would end up as bondage. I have often been asked how to prevent the teaching on grace degenerating into licence and ultimately sin. I understand people's concern. But I wish they would show as much concern for the sin of legalism, which has cursed British Christianity for decades. I believe that legalism and licence are equally abominable to God. If Satan cannot get you into licence, he will try and get you into legalism.

'The only antidote to both is good sound Bible teaching, though I don't particularly like that term because it is often used by evangelicals to pull people back into the legalist camp. But if we can have really anointed Bible teachers, and can ensure that Christians hunger after the word of God while staying full of the Holy Spirit, then as long as they are part of a vibrant church they should be able to avoid the trap of legalism. My friend Maurice Smith used to say, 'We have to trust the Holy Spirit.' That's not to say that we don't need to teach believers. But we do have to teach them to walk and live by the Spirit. Bible teaching has a role to play in this, but it is no substitute for it.

'One of the criticisms made of us is that we have never had a tenet of faith like other churches. There is no set of beliefs that people have to sign when they join. But what is the point in the Anglicans having the Thirty-nine Articles when many of their ministers clearly and openly refute them? Or the Pentecostal denominations having fundamental truths which are not fundamental to some of their church leaders? On the one hand, such statements become devalued; on the other, debate and genuine concern for truth are stifled. Our security must never be in our tenets of faith: it can only be in God. Perhaps the pendulum did swing a little too far,

but it was a risk we had to take in order to get it to
move at all.'

Opposite directions

Little did John realise following the 1978 split, that within a
few years he would tread the path of schism again, but this
time nearer to home. As the Romford-based fellowship
grew to a numerical strength of 400–500, the decision was
taken to decentralise into smaller groups while retaining
overall cohesion and authority. It proved to be the pathway
to yet another split as a substantial proportion of the
congregation left the church, following doctrinal differences
between Maurice Smith and John. It came to a head when
John felt that he had to challenge the influence within the
church of Maurice's teaching. John and Maurice had been
together for twelve years, and while John pointedly refers
to his erstwhile colleague as 'my dear friend', it is clear that
nearly a decade later, neither John himself nor the work in
Romford has fully recovered. The quietness of John's voice
as he shares concerning that period, seems to betray a sense
of deep emotion.

'We probably gave away authority too quickly after decen-
tralising. But at that time we were moving on the crest of
a wave, and didn't realise the need of instituting a certain
amount of structure into what we were doing. Our lack
of structure became the vehicle by which error was able
to spread so rapidly. Everything we did was based on
relationship and friendship. It's a mistake many other
fellowships have made since.

'We were left with about 60 per cent of the people. Those
who remained kept in a relationship with each other and
with me. Norman Barnes for example continued to meet
in Chadwell Heath, and kept in touch with other groups in

Romford, Barking and one or two other places. I'm glad to say that with the passage of time, relationships with some of those who pulled away at that time have been restored, including with Dave Bilborough and John Menlove who were an integral part of our worship team.'

For some time now part of the work in the Essex area has been spearheaded by Dave Matthews, with an emphasis on bringing together churches in the region for celebration, evangelism and co-operation in world mission. Ironically it's a strategy that John first sought to implement, though without success, in those heady days of the early 1960s. At the time of writing plans were still afoot for John and Christine's move to the Cobham area to facilitate their new roles in Pioneer alongside Gerald Coates. Whether the two men, close friends admittedly, succeed in establishing a close working relationship will become clear with the passage of time. Relationships between leaders in the house churches have been as difficult to maintain as in the denominations. But at a time of life when many people would be seeking to take things more slowly, John is fuelled up with enthusiasm for the new venture, and has made no provision for retirement! While the details have not yet been fully worked out, many of the churches and ministries linked to John's Team Spirit organisation (sorry John, I couldn't think of a better word!) are in the process of merging with Gerald's Pioneer. What is certain however, is the direction that John will take in his ministry over the next few years.

Reaching out

Ironically it was Bryn Jones who during a very rare meeting with John gave him a prophetic word. It was that God had called him to serve the wider church, and that he was not to get himself locked in exclusively to the new-church movement. Shortly afterwards John was approached by a group of Catholic believers with a view to holding some joint meetings in Westminster Central Hall. It was to be the beginning of an ongoing relationship that has developed since. John was involved in the Bern Conference which brought Christians from thirty countries together for teaching, worship and fellowship. Some 50 per cent of those attending were from non-Protestant groups. He was involved too in Brighton 91, which involved leaders from most countries and denominations of the world.

The second thing that happened was an invitation for John and Christine to speak at Spring Harvest. For the last ten years they have become almost part of the furniture at the interdenominational event. Could it be that the man who wrote a booklet called *Forgive us our Denominations* is losing his radical edge? John admits that there has been no shortage of suggestions to that effect.

'What I actually said in the booklet was that denominationalism is a sin. I went on to say that the worst kind of sectarianism is to say, "I am of Christ", which is precisely what some of the new churches were doing. I have never had a problem with a person being in, and feeling called to a denomination. My difficulty is with those who while not claiming that their denomination is the only denomination, act as if it was!

'We have been seriously criticised for reaching out to the denominations by some in the new churches who have claimed we were compromising. But far from losing our radical edge, I feel that it is our critics who are in fact guilty of that. In my understanding, being radical is doing what God is telling you to do now. Continuing to pursue yesterday's agenda is not radicalism. I personally feel called today to relate to those who have captured the vision for something better than any of us have at present.'

Full circle

'I always felt that the house churches had been raised up by the Lord not simply to become another movement, but to act as a catalyst and a spur to other Christians. In the early days we got boxed in partly as a result of our own arrogance, and partly by being isolated by those who shut their doors to us. But God is bigger than our weaknesses, and he has brought us now to the place where things have turned full circle. The massive growth in new churches has in my opinion acted as a gauntlet to many denominations to get their act together. There are very encouraging signs in many of them. For example the Salvation Army is now putting all its officers through church growth courses, and almost all the denominations including the Pentecostals are setting church planting goals. I visualise an increase of this over the next few years as churches come together, while still retaining their denominational links and distinctives. There are still some barriers that must come down, especially in terms of autonomy and blind loyalty to one's own particular brand label. But I believe that will come in God's time and as trust between believers is established.'

But what of the house churches themselves? It is of course impossible to generalise among such a diverse group. What is clear however, at least to men like John, is that they are not immune to the lessons of history. Unless they respond to the changing face of evangelicalism, he argues, the new could quickly become the old.

'Statistics on church growth only tell you what happened yesterday. The new churches would do well to remember the adage that yesterday's radicals usually become today's reactionaries. I feel that there are many new churches which have adopted an attitude of smug self-satisfaction, allied to a refusal to hear from God today. They are no longer committed to relating to other groups of believers, are not exposed to such events as Spring Harvest and as a result are becoming almost cultic. I can see such churches becoming relics in the 1990s.'

End-time battle

'One of the distinctives of new churches right from our early origins has been our positive view of eschatology. I have never lost that. I feel certain that something very significant is happening at present in the spiritual atmosphere of our nation and indeed of the world. The relationships that are being put into place in this decade of evangelism are being duplicated by Satan and his followers. Things are coming to a head in the battle for the earth at the end of the age.

'God is putting together his kind of a church, based on relationships, that will ensure that he has a powerful witness in every nation on earth. I have never changed my beliefs on this, but I have seen and become part of a change of emphasis. In fact I am deeply thankful to God that he has allowed and helped me to make the transition into what he is doing today.

'Some years ago the Lord gave me a picture of a receding tide which was linked to the passage of church history. I interpreted it, that after his ministry was completed, Jesus went back to heaven and left a group of apostles who themselves did an amazing job. But this was soon taken over by administrators, who administrated the prophets out of the situation. Before long we had a Bible that no one could understand, and we went into the Dark

Ages. Then I came to see that over a period of time
since then, the reverse has taken place. The Bible was
put into the language of ordinary people, the teaching
ministry restored to the church, and the era of the great
evangelists came into being. Latterly we have focused
once again on the prophetic and apostolic ministries. In
other words, church history has come full circle. Now
before people get too excited about the final step, which
is of course the reversal of Jesus going back to heaven, let
me add that we're not quite there yet!'

Vital gifts

'I don't think we have yet focused enough on apostles and
prophets. In my opinion, they will be vital to the emerging
of the calibre of church that will be needed in the last days.
They will not do the work of the church, but will do God's
work in the church. In this way, God's work in the world
will become possible. I have relationships now with most
of the denominational leaders, though obviously at varying
levels. And I see emerging in most of the denominations,
men and women who I would describe as apostolic and
prophetic, even though they might use different terms.'

According to John these gifts are not simply emerging
throughout the church; they are also beginning to 'network'. That is a concept which is increasingly being advo-
cated and one which is clearly very close to John's heart.
It involves the Ephesians 4 gifts, not only recognising and
confirming each other's ministries in a non-competitive
way, but also drawing strength from each other through
close relationships. There is a glint in John's eyes as
he contemplates the prospect of that coming to pass.
In spite of having experienced first-hand the pain of
broken relationships, John has never lost his belief in their

crucial importance. The illustration he uses to reinforce the concept of networking is a significant one.

'The strands of a net are both horizontal and vertical. Networking with other people provides the horizontal strength that might otherwise lead to the fish getting away. So I believe that the kind of networking that is going on today, and in which I am delighted to play a role, will be a vital ingredient of the net with which the Lord will bring in the final draft of fish before Jesus comes.'

Signs and wonders

'For that to happen, we will also need an outpouring of signs and wonders. We are simply not going to reach the multitudes of this needy world without signs and wonders. They were an intrinsic part of Jesus' ministry, and that of the apostles. How can we possibly think that we can do the job with blunt tools? We have majored in Britain on character, while in the USA the emphasis has been more on power. That has been the difference between us, with the result that neither of us has done much. The two aspects of the arrow, that is the straight shaft and the sharp tip, have to come together. Similarly many of the Two-thirds World countries have experienced an outpouring of power, but are woefully weak in places on Bible teaching.

'That is where networking on a mutual basis can play an important part. Ministries will be able to move between churches and nations within the security and trust of relationships. House churches have always talked about God's hidden agenda, his unseen activity behind the scenes. I believe that God has been putting what I can only describe as a new electricity system into the church. Networking is part of that system. All the channelling is being put into place, as are the plugs and the wiring.

'At some point in history, when he is ready, God will connect up all this infrastructure into a fuse box, and switch on. Then I believe the earth will light up with the glory of the Lord in a way that none of us has seen before. The results should be electric!'

A Final Word

In less than five years' time there will no doubt be a surge of books recording the history of British Christianity within the last 1,000 years. They will show that the nineteenth century was the era of the great preachers, the rise of the missionary societies, and the pre-eminence of the person of Jesus Christ.

In the twentieth century however, we have seen the re-emergence of the third person of the Trinity to a place of importance in the church's agenda.

Without over-emphasising the distinction between the three persons of the Godhead, and thereby falling into an age-old doctrinal trap, it is fair to say that this century has been a season of the Spirit. Starting with the Welsh revival at its dawn, continuing with the rise of the Pentecostal movement, and culminating in the ongoing charismatic renewal, many groups in the church of Jesus Christ have experienced an unparalleled outpouring of the Holy Spirit. This has had the effect of revolutionising the lives of individual believers and transforming the worship and life of congregations.

Within the broad umbrella of the charismatic movement, the emergence of the 'house' or 'new' churches has been a significant development. There can be little doubt that this diverse group of churches, now numbering tens of thousands of Christians and containing many of the largest churches in the country, was raised up by God; or that its influence on British Christianity has been highly significant.

Like all new evangelical movements, it arrived on the scene with a distinctive emphasis which it sought to highlight. And typical of new groups, a clarion call to get back to the Bible was high on its agenda.

But unlike most other new groups, the new churches have within the lifetime of their first generation of leaders evolved beyond recognition: so much so that they have by and large managed to avoid the tendency of new groups to become insular and even cultic. Rather than waiting until 'the generation of Joshua' arises in order to spill its blessings and insights into the wider body of God's people, the new churches have succeeded in exercising considerable influence within the British church scene in just twenty-five years. Witness the many national ministries in word and worship, the number of influential projects and evangelical positions that are now filled by new-church members.

The reason for this is undoubtedly due, in part at least, to the quality of its first generation leaders, many of whom have become household names. Unelected by a voting system, and uncluttered by denominational procedures or narrow doctrinal statements, they have depended totally on their gifting and anointing to forge lasting relationships with other Christians and churches. Many now function in non-threatening relationships, bringing guidance, wisdom and impetus into their associated churches. It is a pattern that would surely have appealed to the Apostle Paul himself. Not a committee in sight!

The enormous growth and popularity of the new churches shows clearly that their time was right. Not just another denomination, nor merely a distinctive truth, but a different kind of church which by its very nature has challenged every other church in the land. The house churches, and particularly their leaders, touched a chord in many Christians as they verbalised what was wrong and debilitating in the twentieth-century church.

Not that house churches are perfect. Or their leaders. With hindsight, many now recognise the sins of pride and obstinacy which produced a highly damaging and hurtful division among the leaders in the mid-1970s. That simply makes them human. They are not saints – at least in the non-biblical sense! Christians need to realise that their leaders are made of clay. They bring with them into their pulpits all the weaknesses that characterise humankind, plus others that are peculiar to their gifting. The story of the new-church leaders over a quarter of a century shows that human frailty is not a disqualification for the service of God. On the contrary, it is an absolute requirement. At a time when the Holy Spirit needed a job doing, a statement making, an established church shaking, he found men who were ready and willing.

But it also teaches us an important lesson about the grace of God. He doesn't give up on us, nor does he reject the clay because of a flaw in its make-up. God is bigger than our failures. It was so with Peter and John in the New Testament, and it still is so with today's Peter and John – and Terry, and Gerald, and Bryn . . .

Healed relationships tend to be stronger than their original counterparts. Time will tell whether those reborn links between most of the new-church leaders will prosper. I believe they will, given that the passage of time and the lessons of failure are valuable teachers. No one would pretend, certainly not the leaders themselves, that the new churches have a monopoly of God's truth and revelation. Their present willingness to work alongside other churches and denominations bears testimony to a welcome humility, which has served to break down much of the suspicion and hostility with which new churches were once greeted. This in turn will surely serve to increase the influence of new churches in general. Who can doubt that this is indeed God's intention. It is now clear that God is neither anti-denominations, nor pro-'new' church. He is merely passionate about a world that needs rescuing from sin, and broken-hearted about a church that for nearly 2,000 years has had all the tools to do the job, but which has so often failed miserably.

The Restorationist teaching that undergirds so many new churches is convinced that the greatest days of the church lie ahead, and that God has been actively preparing his church for those meteoric times. The new churches have certainly been part of that preparation. The rest of us should be thankful.

SALT

GOODNESS & GRACE

SALT

Mary Drum (B.Th)

GRACE

INTRODUCTION

Grace is god's Own loving kindness and favour toward human beings, given freely so we can respond to his call to become children of God. Grace is participation in the life of God.

SALT: GOODNESS & GRACE

Salt is used to bring out flavour and to preserve food and, as such, it helps us to understand how faith enhances our lives. From ages past, salt has been a favourite image used by the writers of Scripture. There is no point in being salt that does not flavour and, similarly, there is no point in being a light that does not brighten. People of faith must taste of their faith and let their light shine. They must add flavour and light to the world and so preserve and enhance all that is good.

Some time ago I was asked to speak to a group of Christian young adults. They came from all walks of life and work experiences but could speak about their faith only with some difficulty. Among them, for instance, I found a young woman who was afraid to tell her work colleagues that she was going to attend a spiritual retreat weekend with other young people. While she had great faith in God, nevertheless, she was afraid to let the light of her faith shine in our pluralist world. It was while I was preparing to talk to these young adults that SALT came to be. And what came to be was a way of thinking which had developed through my years of study and which made sense of my faith and the world within which I practised it.

Life is creation, a gift of loving kindness from God. And this gift – this very act of creation – places us in relationship to God. We respond to our Creator in good faith by being good. Faith requires time for prayer and contemplation to help us name and ever more fully to understand our gifts, what it is we believe and what it is we are to do. From faith and prayer too we can hope for a good life today and tomorrow.

Being good, though, is not enough. We are required to *do* good. The relationship we have with God also places us in relationship to the rest of creation, that is, with all the people and the natural environment that are parts of the great work of creation. All living creatures have the right to life according to their own ecological niche but every human being has the right to hope for a good life. We, human beings, are God's stewards of creation.

It will always be on our consciences or our hearts how we answer to God for our works. We need to work hard to inform our consciences to help us to make good decisions. We can do this through practising good works in faith and by lives of prayer as we respond to the gift of life given in loving kindness.

Mt 5:13–16

Matthew 5:13-16
"You are the salt of the earth.
But if the salt loses its saltiness,
how can it be made salty
again? It is no longer good for
anything, except to be thrown
out and trampled by men.

You are the light of the world.
A city on a hill cannot be
hidden.

Neither do people light a
lamp and put it under a bowl.
Instead they put it on its stand,
and it gives light to everyone
in the house.

In the same way, let your light
shine before men, that they
may see your good deeds
and praise your Father in
heaven."

LIFE

When God makes us, he leaves a trace of himself in our hearts so that we may know him and his goodness and kindness. This trace we see echoed in all the created world and its people. They are our sounding board for the echoes in our own hearts.

GE 1:26

PSALM 119:73
Your hands made me and
formed me; give me
understanding to learn
your commands.

DEUTERONOMY 7:7-8

The LORD did not set his affection on you and choose you because you were more numerous than other peoples, for you were the fewest of all peoples. But it was because the LORD loved you and kept the oath he swore to your forefathers that he brought you out with a mighty hand and redeemed you from the land of slavery, from the power of Pharaoh king of Egypt.

PSALM 139:13-14
For you created my inmost being; you knit me together in my mother's womb. I praise you because I am fearfully and wonderfully made; your works are wonderful, I know that full well.

PHILIPPIANS 4:7
And the peace of God, which
transcends all understanding,
will guard your hearts and your
minds in Christ Jesus.

PHIL 4:8

PHILIPPIANS 4:8
Finally, brothers, whatever is
true, whatever is noble,
whatever is right, whatever is
pure, whatever is lovely,
whatever is admirable – if
anything is excellent or
praiseworthy – think about
such things.

Isaiah 64:8
Yet, O LORD, you are our
Father. We are the clay, you
are the potter; we are all the
work of your hand.

FAITH

From ages past, human beings have asked questions, such as: What are we? And: What gives our lives meaning? Such questions reveal the restlessness in our hearts and they demand answers. By our very nature, we quest for understanding.

The answers to our questions lie in discovering ever more deeply the existence of other living beings in creation, especially other human beings. The other echoes in our hearts; we recognise ourselves in the other.

Human beings have the freedom to question and to seek understanding, and faith can be our way of responding, in freedom, to God's revelation. We can choose to respond to God. While freedom opens the way to accepting responsibility, faith helps us better to exercise it.

Abraham was the father of three great faiths: Judaism, Christianity and Islam. In the New Testament, we see exceptional examples of faith among Jesus' disciples when they leave their fishing nets behind to take on the new work of the Lord. This new work – of spreading the good news of the reign of God's love – is the mission of God's new pilgrim people, the Church.

Faith motivates us to seek direction by the Holy Spirit. Faith is a vocation and we come fully alive by living with it. Faith is a virtue.

GALATIANS 3:25-26
Now that faith has come, we
are no longer under the
supervision of the law. You are
all sons of God through faith in
Christ Jesus.

HEBREWS 11:8-10

By faith Abraham, when called
to go to a place he would
later receive as his
inheritance, obeyed and
went, even though he did not
know where he was going. By
faith he made his home in the
promised land like a stranger
in a foreign country; he lived
in tents, as did Isaac and
Jacob, who were heirs with
him of the same promise. For
he was looking forward to the
city with foundations, whose
architect and builder is God.

ACTS 11:24
He was a good man, full of
the Holy Spirit and faith, and
a great number of people
were brought to the Lord.

LUKE 1:38

LUKE 1:38
"I am the LORD's servant,"
Mary answered. "May it be to
me as you have said." Then
the angel left her.

LUKE 17:5

The apostles said to the Lord,
"Increase our faith!"

2 TIMOTHY 3:15
"and how from infancy you
have known the Holy
Scriptures, which are able to
make you wise for salvation,
through faith in Christ Jesus."

JOHN 3:8
"The wind blows wherever it pleases. You hear its sound, but you cannot tell where it comes from or where it is going. So it is with everyone born of the Spirit."

That everyone who believes in him
may have eternal life.

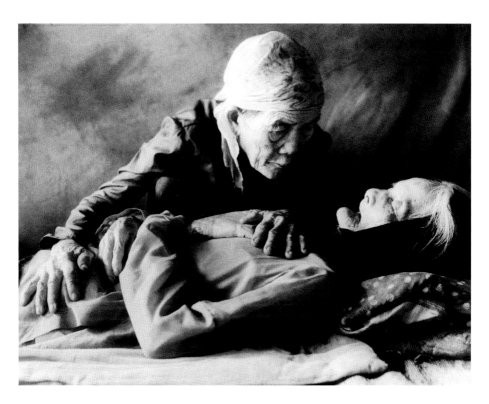

JOHN 3:15

JOHN 15:7-8
If you remain in me and
my words remain in you, ask
whatever you wish, and it will
be given you. This is to my
Father's glory, that you bear
much fruit, showing yourselves
to be my disciples.

MT 15:28

MATTHEW 15:28
Then Jesus answered,
"Woman, you have great faith!
Your request is granted." And
her daughter was healed from
that very hour.

Mᴋ 1:17–18

Mark 1:17-18
"Come, follow me," Jesus said,
"and I will make you fishers of
men."
At once they left their nets
and followed him.

HOPE

ROMANS 4:18 Against all hope, Abraham in hope believed and so became the father of many nations, just as it had been said to him, "So shall your offspring be."

Because of faith, we have hope for a future which we can enjoy even now: eternal life. Hope is a virtue. And just as Abraham was the father of faith, so too, from him, can we learn the lesson of hope.

In faith we contemplate all the gifts that God, in his providence, gives us. How can we then, as people of faith, not place all our hope in God?

MATTHEW 6:25-34

"Therefore I tell you, do not worry about your life, what you will eat or drink; or about your body, what you will wear. Is not life more important than food, and the body more important than clothes? Look at the birds of the air; they do not sow or reap or store away in barns, and yet your heavenly Father feeds them. Are you not much more valuable than they? Who of you by worrying can add a single hour to his life?

"And why do you worry about clothes? See how the lilies of the field grow. They do not labour or spin. Yet I tell you that not even Solomon in all his splendour was dressed like one of these. If that is how God clothes the grass of the field, which is here today and tomorrow is thrown into the fire, will he not much more clothe you, O you of little faith? So do not worry, saying, 'What shall we eat?' or 'What shall we drink?' or 'What shall we wear?'

For the pagans run after all these things, and your heavenly Father knows that you need them. But seek first his kingdom and his righteousness, and all these things will be given to you as well. Therefore do not worry about tomorrow, for tomorrow will worry about itself. Each day has enough trouble of its own."

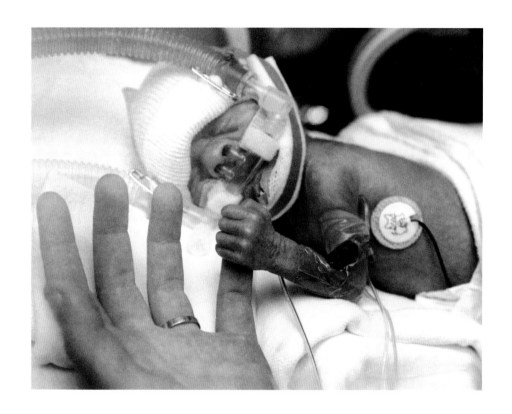

MT 5:1–12

MATTHEW 5:1-12

Now when he saw the crowds, he went up on a mountainside and sat down. His disciples came to him, and he began to teach them, saying:

"Blessed are the poor in spirit, for theirs is the kingdom of heaven. Blessed are those who mourn, for they will be comforted. Blessed are the meek, for they will inherit the earth. Blessed are those who hunger and thirst for righteousness, for they will be filled. Blessed are the merciful, for they will be shown mercy. Blessed are the pure in heart, for they will see God. Blessed are the peacemakers, for they will be called sons of God. Blessed are those who are persecuted because of righteousness, for theirs is the kingdom of heaven.

"Blessed are you when people insult you, persecute you and falsely say all kinds of evil against you because of me. Rejoice and be glad, because great is your reward in heaven, for in the same way they persecuted the prophets who were before you."

Ro 8:31

ROMANS 8:31
What, then, shall we say in response to this? If God is for us, who can be against us?

HEBREWS 11:1
Now faith is being sure of what
we hope for and certain of
what we do not see.

61

PSALM 1:3
He is like a tree planted by
streams of water, which yields
its fruit in season and whose
leaf does not wither.
Whatever he does prospers.

PS 103:1-22

Ps 103:1-22

Praise the LORD, O my soul;
all my inmost being, praise his
holy name.

Praise the LORD, O my soul,
and forget not all his benefits –
who forgives all your sins and
heals all your diseases, who
redeems your life from the pit
and crowns you with love and
compassion, who satisfies your
desires with good things so
that your youth is renewed like
the eagle's.

The LORD works
righteousness and justice for
all the oppressed.

He made known his ways
to Moses, his deeds to the
people of Israel: The LORD is
compassionate and gracious,
slow to anger, abounding
in love.

He will not always accuse,
nor will he harbour his anger
forever; he does not treat us
as our sins deserve or repay us
according to our iniquities.

For as high as the heavens are
above the earth, so great is his
love for those who fear him; as
far as the east is from the west,
so far has he removed our
transgressions from us.

As a father has compassion
on his children, so the LORD
has compassion on those who
fear him; for he knows how we
are formed, he remembers
that we are dust.

As for man, his days are like
grass, he flourishes like a flower
of the field; the wind blows
over it and it is gone, and its
place remembers it
no more.

But from everlasting to
everlasting the LORD'S love is
with those who fear him, and
his righteousness with their
children's children with those
who keep his covenant
and remember to obey
his precepts.

The LORD has established his
throne in heaven, and his
kingdom rules over all.

Praise the LORD, you his
angels, you mighty ones who
do his bidding, who obey
his word.

Praise the LORD, all his
heavenly hosts, you his
servants who do his will.

Praise the LORD, all his works
everywhere in his dominion.
Praise the LORD, O my soul.

JOHN 10:10
I have come that they may
have life, and have it to
the full.

PSALM 34:8
Taste and see that the LORD is good; blessed is the man who takes refuge in him.

PSALM 34:18
The LORD is close to the
brokenhearted and saves
those who are crushed in
spirit.

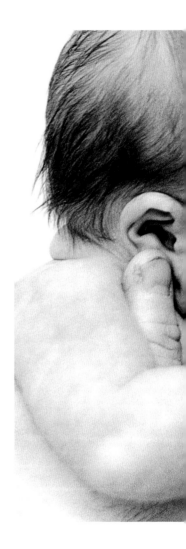

ROMANS 15:13
May the God of hope fill you
with all joy and peace as you
trust in him.

RO 15:13

For in this hope we were saved. But hope that is seen is no hope at all. Who hopes for what he already has?

But if we hope for what we do not yet have, we wait for it patiently.

PSALM 138:1-8

I will praise you, O LORD, with
all my heart; before the
"gods" I will sing your praise.

I will bow down toward your
holy temple and will praise
your name for your love and
your faithfulness, for you have
exalted above all things your
name and your word.

When I called, you answered
me; you made me bold and
stouthearted.

May all the kings of the
earth praise you, O LORD,
when they hear the words
of your mouth.

May they sing of the ways of
the LORD, for the glory of the
LORD is great.

Though the LORD is on high,
he looks upon the lowly, but
the proud he knows from afar.

Though I walk in the midst of
trouble, you preserve my life;
you stretch out your hand
against the anger of my foes,
with your right hand you
save me.

The LORD will fulfill his
purpose for me; your love,
O LORD, endures forever –
do not abandon the works
of your hands.

ECC 9:4

ECCLESIASTES 9:4
Anyone who is among the living has hope even a live dog is better off than a dead lion!

PSALM 33:22 May your unfailing love rest upon us, O LORD, even as we put our hope in you.

PROVERBS 28:20
A faithful man will be
richly blessed.

PRAYER

MARK 1:35 Very early in the morning, while it was still dark, Jesus got up, left the house and went off to a solitary place, where he prayed.

Our divine and human Lord, Jesus, shows us that prayer is necessary. In prayer we connect with God and, through God, with those for whom we pray. We are not alone. In prayer we give thanks and we are given what it is needed: in prayer we receive love through grace. Jesus shows us that prayer and faith are inseparable, that prayer is a necessity and that it is always possible to pray. In prayer we ask the Holy Spirit to guide us and continue our lessons in wisdom. Prayer brings together two of the great theological virtues: faith and hope. In prayer we lift our minds to God and his ways.

Mт 6:5-15

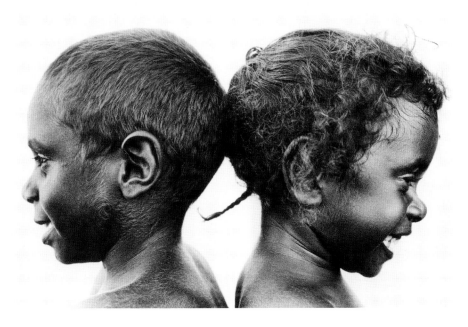

MATTHEW 6:5-15

"And when you pray, do not be like the hypocrites, for they love to pray standing in the synagogues and on the street corners to be seen by men. I tell you the truth, they have received their reward in full. But when you pray, go into your room, close the door and pray to your Father, who is unseen. Then your Father, who sees what is done in secret, will reward you. And when

you pray, do not keep on babbling like pagans, for they think they will be heard because of their many words. Do not be like them, for your Father knows what you need before you ask him.

"This, then, is how you should pray: 'Our Father in heaven, hallowed be your name, your kingdom come, your will be done on earth as it is in

heaven. Give us today our daily bread. Forgive us our debts, as we also have forgiven our debtors. And lead us not into temptation, but deliver us from the evil one.' For if you forgive men when they sin against you, your heavenly Father will also forgive you. But if you do not forgive men their sins, your Father will not forgive your sins."

PSALM 119:27
Let me understand the
teaching of your precepts;
then I will meditate on
your wonders.

COLOSSIANS 4:12
Epaphras, who is one of you
and a servant of Christ Jesus,
sends greetings. He is always
wrestling in prayer for you, that
you may stand firm in all the
will of God, mature and fully
assured.

COL 4:12

ROMANS 8:26
In the same way, the Spirit
helps us in our weakness. We
do not know what we ought
to pray for, but the Spirit
himself intercedes for us
with groans that words
cannot express.

JEREMIAH 29:13
You will seek me and find me
when you seek me with all
your heart.

ISAIAH 55:3,6

Give ear and come to me;
hear me, that your soul may
live. I will make an everlasting
covenant with you, my faithful
love promised to David.

...

Seek the Lord while he may
be found; call on him while he
is near.

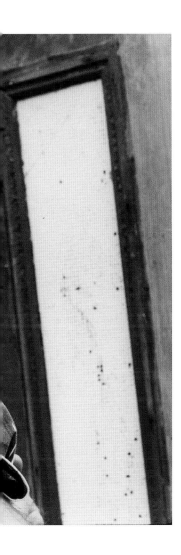

1 JOHN 5:14
This is the confidence we have
in approaching God: that if
we ask anything according to
his will, he hears us.

Luke 11:9-13
"So I say to you: Ask and it will be given to you; seek and you will find; knock and the door will be opened to you.

"For everyone who asks receives; he who seeks finds; and to him who knocks, the door will be opened.

"Which of you fathers, if your son asks for a fish, will give him a snake instead? Or if he asks for an egg, will give him a scorpion?

"If you then, though you are evil, know how to give good gifts to your children, how much more will your Father in heaven give the Holy Spirit to those who ask him!"

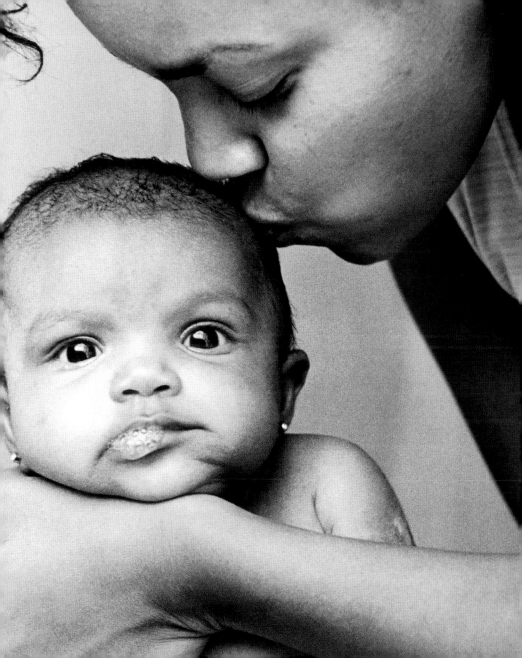

Ps 34:1-7

Psalm 34:1-7

I will extol the LORD at all times; his praise will always be on my lips. My soul will boast in the LORD; let the afflicted hear and rejoice. Glorify the LORD with me; let us exalt his name together. I sought the LORD, and he answered me; he delivered me from all my fears.

Those who look to him are radiant; their faces are never covered with shame. This poor man called, and the LORD heard him; he saved him out of all his troubles. The angel of the LORD encamps around those who fear him, and he delivers them.

1 John 5:15
And if we know that he hears
us – whatever we ask – we
know that we have what we
asked of him.

PSALM 143:1
O LORD, hear my prayer, listen
to my cry for mercy; in your
faithfulness and righteousness
come to my relief.

PSALM 4:1
Answer me when I call to you,
O my righteous God. Give me
relief from my distress; be
merciful to me and hear
my prayer.

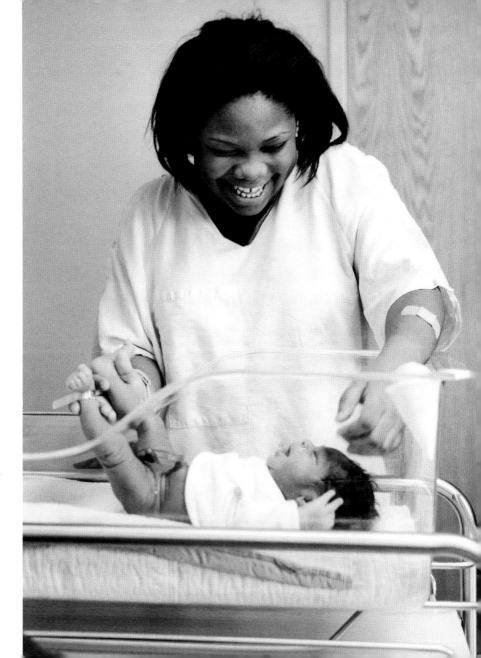

EPH 1:15-19

EPHESIANS 1:15-19

For this reason, ever since I heard about your faith in the Lord Jesus and your love for all the saints, I have not stopped giving thanks for you, remembering you in my prayers. I keep asking that the God of our Lord Jesus Christ, the glorious Father, may give you the Spirit of wisdom and revelation, so that you may know him better. I pray also that the eyes of your heart may be enlightened in order that you may know the hope to which he has called you, the riches of his glorious inheritance in the saints, and his incomparably great power for us who believe. That power is like the working of his mighty strength.

CONSCIENCE

ROMANS 2:15 Since they show that the requirements of the law are written on their hearts, their consciences also bearing witness, and their thoughts now accusing, now even defending them.

Conscience lies at the foundation of every religion. In our conscience – our heart of hearts – is the echo of the other, the rest of creation. Conscience does not consist in false guilt but it can give rise to feelings of true guilt when we honestly acknowledge that we have done wrong or avoided doing good.

It is within us to seek a good life and it is the virtues that are the muscles that exercise our conscience. We need the virtues of faith, hope and love to live a good life. A person who has a conscience puts conscience at the centre of their being; they aspire to being good and they do good.

A conscience requires imagination and the ability to think of the good that is possible. The saints, including the martyrs, are superlative examples for us to follow. During the course of their biological lives they were moved by faith to act with love.

But note that acting on our initiative from an informed conscience does not mean acting in isolation. When we act in good conscience, we participate in the life of the other, and, what is more, we build up the other and ourselves. We become who we are destined to be – in loving relationship to the other; and the other becomes who they are destined to be – in loving relationship to us.

Hebrews 13:18
Pray for us. We are sure that
we have a clear conscience
and desire to live honou--rably
in every way.

2 CORINTHIANS 1:12
Now this is our boast: Our
conscience testifies that we
have conducted ourselves in
the world, and especially in
our relations with you, in the
holiness and sincerity that are
from God. We have done so
not according to worldly
wisdom but according to
God's grace.

ROMANS 14:11-13
It is written: 'As surely as I live,' says the Lord, 'every knee will bow before me; every tongue will confess to God.' So then, each of us will give an account of himself to God.

Therefore let us stop passing judgment on one another. Instead, make up your mind not to put any stumbling block or obstacle in your brother's way.

1 Co 10:24

1 CORINTHIANS 10:24
Nobody should seek his own
good, but the good of others.

HOSEA 14:9

Who is wise? He will realise
these things. Who is
discerning? He will understand
them. The ways of the LORD
are right; the righteous walk in
them, but the rebellious
stumble in them.

ECCLESIASTES 12:13
Now all has been heard;
here is the conclusion of the
matter: Fear God and keep
his commandments, for this is
the whole duty of man.

2 CORINTHIANS 4:2

Rather, we have renounced secret and shameful ways; we do not use deception, nor do we distort the word of God. On the contrary, by setting forth the truth plainly we commend ourselves to every man's conscience in the sight of God.

I will give you a new heart
and put a new spirit in you;
I will remove from you your
heart of stone and give you
a heart of flesh.

And I will put my Spirit in you
and move you to follow my
decrees and be careful to
keep my laws.

PSALM 139:23-24
Search me, O God, and know
my heart; test me and know
my anxious thoughts.

See if there is any offensive
way in me, and lead me in the
way everlasting.

ROMANS 13:5-7
Therefore, it is necessary to submit to the authorities, not only because of possible punishment but also because of conscience.

This is also why you pay taxes, for the authorities are God's servants, who give their full time to governing.

Give everyone what you owe him: If you owe taxes, pay taxes; if revenue, then revenue; if respect, then respect; if honour, then honour.

PSALM 37:23-24
If the LORD delights in a man's
way, he makes his steps firm;
though he stumble, he will not
fall, for the LORD upholds him
with his hand.

Ps 51:10-12

PSALM 51:10-12
Create in me a pure heart,
O God, and renew a steadfast
spirit within me.

Do not cast me from your
presence or take your Holy
Spirit from me.

Restore to me the joy of your
salvation and grant me a
willing spirit, to sustain me.

GAL 5:22-26

GALATIANS 5:22-26

But the fruit of the Spirit is love, joy, peace, patience, kindness, goodness, faithfulness, gentleness and self-control. Against such things there is no law. Those who belong to Christ Jesus have crucified the sinful nature with its passions and desires. Since we live by the Spirit, let us keep in step with the Spirit. Let us not become conceited, provoking and envying each other.

PSALM 27:13 I am still confident of this:
I will see the goodness of the LORD
in the land of the living.

Acknowledgements

All images in *Salt* were originally published by **M I L K** Publishing Limited and have been used under licence from **M I L K** Licensing Limited, all rights reserved. www.milkphotos.com

The images are Copyright © the individual photographers as follows.

p12 Les Slesnick
pp14-15 Sándor Horváth
p17 and cover Jerry Koontz
p19 Tetsuaki Oda
p21 and cover Jenny Matthews
p22 Charley Van Dugteren
pp24-25 Malie Rich-Griffith
p27 Thanh Long
pp30-31 Jamshid Bayrami
p32 Robert Billington
p35 and cover Desmond Williams
p37 and cover
Lydia Linda Ruscitto
p38 and cover K Hatt
p41 Romualdas Požerskis
pp42-43 Kamthorn
Pongsutiyakorn
p45 and cover Duc Doan
p47 Stefano Azario
p48 Slim Labidi
p51 Lance Jones
p55 Andreas Heumann
p56 Simon Young

p59 Michael Decher
pp61 Eddee Daniel
p62 Auke Vleer
p64 Maňo Štrauch
p66 and cover Lynn Goldsmith
p68 and cover Stacey P Morgan
p70 Jia Lin Wu
p73 Roumualdas Požerskis
pp74-75 Shannon Eckstein
p77 Steven Baldwin
p78 and cover Guan Cheong Wong
p80 Shannon Eckstein
p83 Thierry Des Ouches
pp84-85 Rinaldo Morelli
p89 Steven Siewert
p91 Shauna Angel Blue
p92 Claude Coirault
p94 Peter van Hoof
p97 Darien Mejía-Olivares
p98 Vankata Sunder Rao Pampana
(Sunder)
pp100-101 Jane Wyles
p103 and cover Ário Gonçalves

p104 Cheryl Shoji
p107 Sam Devine Tischler
p109 Claude Coirault
p111 Mark LaRocca
p113 and cover Andrew Danson
pp116-117 and cover
Ricardo Ordóñez
p118 Jenny Jozwiak
p121 and cover Bill Frantz
p123 Lambro (Tsiliyiannis)
p124 Hazel Hankin
p126 Viktor Kolar
p129 Rogério Ribeiro
p130 Guus Rijven
p132 Simon Lynn
pp134-135 Binode Kumar Das
pp136-137 Juan P Barragán
p139 Kris Allan
p140 Noelle Tan
p143 Steven G Smith
p145 Gay Block

Published by St Pauls Publications, PO Box 906, Strathfield NSW 2135 Australia,
www.stpauls.com.au

This edition published in 2007 by St Pauls Publications in association with Drum Publishing Pty
Ltd under license from M.I.L.K. Licensing Ltd. Title and concept Copyright © 2007 Mary
Drum Pty Ltd. The right of Mary Drum to be identified as author of this work has been asserted
by her in accordance with the Copyright, Designs and Patents Act 1988.

British Library Cataloguing Data.
A catalogue record for this book is available from the British Library.

Designed by Carolyn Lewis.
Printed and bound by 1010 Printing International Ltd, China.